Every name has a meaning drawn from the language of its origin. There is more to a name than its literal meaning, however. Each name can and does suggest a character quality— a goal for which to strive.

God has made you a special creation. He wants you to live up to . . .

your name.

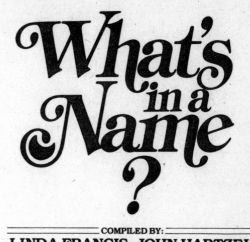

What's in a Name?

COMPILED BY:

LINDA FRANCIS, JOHN HARTZEL
AND
AL PALMQUIST

LIVING BOOKS
Tyndale House Publishers, Inc.
Wheaton, Illinois

Living Books is a registered trademark of Tyndale House Publishers, Inc.

What's in a Name

Tyndale House Publishers, Inc.
Wheaton, Illinois

Published by arrangement with Jeremy Books,
Minneapolis, Minnesota

Copyright © 1976 by Ark Products
All rights reserved

Library of Congress Catalog Card Number 82-50734
ISBN 0-8423-7935-5, Living Books edition

Printed in the United States of America

95 94

18 17

INTRODUCTION

When God plans a project, many lives are touched in the process of its development. This book is no exception. It all started when the Mayor of Minneapolis made an unusual request of an unusual cop. He asked Al Palmquist to set up a rehabilitation program for drug addicts.

Most drug users don't ask policemen to rehabilitate them. They ask Al. Most cops aren't preachers. Al Palmquist is. He knew God loved drug users and wanted to set them free. So he trusted God for the wisdom, the staff, the money; and Midwest Challenge became a reality. (The story of this Christ-centered rehabilitation program is told in Al's book, *Miracle at City Hall*.)

Early in 1974, Midwest Challenge began to investigate new areas of production and vocational training for the young people in its program. John Hartzell, an assistant director for Midwest, proposed making something different in the way of decorative name plaques. They were to be unique, personalized, scriptural. John gave the idea to artist Terry Dugan who designed several prototypes. The plaques were made; the response to them was so enthusiastic, Midwest Challenge organized a new company called ARK Products in order to manufacture and distribute them. Chuck Hetland, Ark's manager, soon realized more people needed to be told the story of the plaques and the philosophy behind them. Chuck talked to Linda Francis, who had been doing research for the project, and it was she who compiled the material for this book.

Most name books give mainly literal or cultural meaning. Some will list beside each entry, famous people having had that name. Some will add quotations from well-known literary works. These books are, in a sense, impersonal name dictionaries and are not intended to be otherwise. This book is different!

Throughout the Bible are countless instances revealing God's interest in individuals and in their names. So deep was this interest, He sometimes changed names in order to better work out His plan in their lives. He's also interested in you. We believe God has made you a special creation. He has a unique life for you. He wants you to live up to the potential He has placed within you. He wants you to live up to your name.

Every name has a meaning drawn from the language of its origin. Sometimes that meaning is obscured because of changes in the culture or in the customs. There is more to a name than its literal meaning, however. Each name can and does suggest a character quality—a goal for which to strive. That's why this book is different. It features your name, the literal meaning, the character quality and an applicable scripture verse. This compilation will help you to understand the significance of your name and inspire you to live up to the character quality it suggests.

Sometimes an explanation has been included to help you realize the relationship between character quality and literal meaning. The name *Beverly*, for example, means "by the beaver dam." Since beavers are known for their industry, Beverly's character quality is *industrious*.

Douglas means "up from the black lagoon." To leave such a place, a person would have to look for the light; therefore, *Seeker of Light* is the character quality assigned.

Included are certain names for which no literal

meanings could be found. In such cases we assigned those character qualities we felt were implied in resource materials available to us.

A young boy overheard an uncle speaking to his father. "I don't know why you named that boy Clayton," the uncle said. "Clay is dirt and that's what his name means—dirt. He'll never amount to anything."

"You could be right," the father replied.

Clayton never forgot that conversation. He hated his name and he hated himself. Subconsciously he began to live up to his conception of the name's meaning. Whenever he experienced failure, he chalked it up to his name. After all, he was just dirt, wasn't he? Clayton grew into manhood feeling worthless.

One day on business he contacted Midwest Challenge. After hearing about the name plaques, he told his story to John Hartzell. John looked through our names to see if Clayton had been researched. It had. He discovered Clayton did refer to clay, but there was a special way to look at it. Clay isn't just dirt. It's an important substance, a raw material; when placed in the potter's hand, it becomes a thing of usefulness and beauty. God compared clay to his own special people. That's why the character quality for Clayton is *In God's Mold* and the verse says, *"... take notice, just as the clay is in the potter's hand, so you are in My hand...."*

That man learned he was unique in God's eyes—that God had special plans for him. As he let God unfold those plans, Clayton became a new person—the person God intended him to be.

Your name is unique and is as important as you are. Let God show you how to live up to it.

THE EDITORS

AARON

Literal Meaning
LIGHT BRINGER
Suggested Character Quality or Godly Characteristic
BRINGER OF LIGHT
Suggested Lifetime Scripture Verse — Psalm 27:1
"The Lord is my light and my salvation; whom shall I fear? The Lord is the strength of my life; of whom shall I be afraid?"

ABBOT

Literal Meaning
FATHER
Suggested Character Quality or Godly Characteristic
BENEVOLENT HEART
Suggested Lifetime Scripture Verse — I Corinthians 13:13
"There remain then, faith, hope, love, these three; but the greatest of these is love."

ABEL

Literal Meaning
BREATH
Suggested Character Quality or Godly Characteristic
FULL OF LIFE
Suggested Lifetime Scripture Verse — Psalm 52:8
"But I am like a green olive tree in the house of God; I trust in God's lovingkindness for ever and ever."

A

ABNER

Literal Meaning
OF LIGHT
Suggested Character Quality or Godly Characteristic
TRUSTWORTHY
Suggested Lifetime Scripture Verse — Psalm 119:44, 45
*"Then I will keep Thy law continually forever and ever
I shall walk with freedom, for I have sought Thy precepts."*

Explanation:
One who is of the light is transparently honest.

ABRAHAM

Literal Meaning
FATHER OF A MULTITUDE
Suggested Character Quality or Godly Characteristic
RIGHTEOUS PROTECTOR
Suggested Lifetime Scripture Verse — Isaiah 64:5
*"Thou dost meet him who is joyful, who works righteously
and who in Thy ways remembers Thee . . ."*

ADA

Literal Meaning
HAPPY
Suggested Character Quality or Godly Characteristic
HAPPY SPIRIT
Suggested Lifetime Scripture Verse — Psalm 5:11
*"But let all who take refuge in Thee rejoice. Let them ever
shout for joy since Thou dost make a covering over them.
Let all who love Thy name be glad in Thee."*

ADAM

Literal Meaning
A MAN OF THE EARTH
Suggested Character Quality or Godly Characteristic
GOD'S CREATION
Suggested Lifetime Scripture Verse — Ephesians 2:10
*"For we are His handiwork, created in Christ Jesus for
good works, which God previously prepared for us so that
we should live in them."*

ADELINE

Literal Meaning
NOBLENESS
Suggested Character Quality or Godly Characteristic
WOMAN OF ESTEEM
Suggested Lifetime Scripture Verse — Hosea 12:6
"So, you return to your God, hold on to love and justice and wait continually on your God."

ADELLA

Literal Meaning
NOBLE
Suggested Character Quality or Godly Characteristic
WOMAN OF ESTEEM
Suggested Lifetime Scripture Verse — Hosea 12:6
"So, you return to your God, hold on to love and justice and wait continually on your God."

ADOLF

Literal Meaning
"NOBLE WOLF"—Germanic
Suggested Character Quality or Godly Characteristic
COURAGEOUS SPIRIT
Suggested Lifetime Scripture Verse — Psalm 34:4
"I sought the Lord and He answered me, and freed me from all my fears."

Explanation:
Noble wolf or hero suggests the ability to meet difficulties bravely.

ADRIAN

Literal Meaning
"BLACK EARTH" — Latin
Suggested Character Quality or Godly Characteristic
CREATIVE HEART
Suggested Lifetime Scripture Verse — Psalm 51:10
"Create in me a clean heart, O God, and renew a steadfast spirit within me."

A

Explanation:
Black earth suggests productivity, a creative ability.

AGATHA

Literal Meaning
GOOD
Suggested Character Quality or Godly Characteristic
A GOOD HEART
Suggested Lifetime Scripture Verse — Ephesians 4:32
"*Be kind toward one another, tenderhearted, forgiving one another, even as God has in Christ forgiven you.*"

AGNES

Literal Meaning
PURE ONE
Suggested Character Quality or Godly Characteristic
PURE ONE
Suggested Lifetime Scripture Verse — Psalm 51:6
"*Surely, Thou desirest truth in the inner self, and Thou makest me to understand hidden wisdom.*"

AIMEE

Literal Meaning
BELOVED ONE
Suggested Character Quality or Godly Characteristic
BELOVED
Suggested Lifetime Scripture Verse — Song of Solomon 2:4
"*He has brought me into the banqueting hall, and His banner over me is love.*"

AL

Literal Meaning
CHEERFUL
Suggested Character Quality or Godly Characteristic
CHEERFUL ONE
Suggested Lifetime Scripture Verse — Jeremiah 15:16
"*Thy words were found, and I ate them, and Thy words were to me a joy and a rejoicing of my heart; for I bear Thy name, O Lord, God of hosts.*"

ALAN

Literal Meaning
HANDSOME, CHEERFUL, HARMONIOUS ONE
Suggested Character Quality or Godly Characteristic
CHEERFUL ONE
Suggested Lifetime Scripture Verse — Jeremiah 15:16
"Thy words were found, and I ate them, and Thy words were to me a joy and a rejoicing of my heart; for I bear Thy name, O Lord, God of hosts."

ALBERT

Literal Meaning
NOBLE, BRILLIANT OR INDUSTRIOUS
Suggested Character Quality or Godly Characteristic
MAN OF HONOR
Suggested Lifetime Scripture Verse — Isaiah 30:18
"Nevertheless the Lord longs to be gracious to you! Therefore He shall rise up to bestow mercy on you; for the Lord is a God of justice. Blessed are they who wait for Him."

ALDEN

Literal Meaning
OLD WISE PROTECTOR OR FRIEND
Suggested Character Quality or Godly Characteristic
FRIENDLY ONE
Suggested Lifetime Scripture Verse — Proverbs 11:30
"The fruit of the righteous is a tree of life, and a wise man wins friends."

ALDRICH

Literal Meaning
WISE RULER
Suggested Character Quality or Godly Characteristic
FULL OF WISDOM
Suggested Lifetime Scripture Verse — Psalm 111:10
"For reverence of the Lord is the beginning of wisdom. There is insight in all who observe it. His praise is everlasting."

A

ALEC

Literal Meaning
"PROTECTING MEN" — Greek
Suggested Character Quality or Godly Characteristic
BRAVE PROTECTOR
Suggested Lifetime Scripture Verse — Psalm 31:24
"Be strong and let your heart take courage, all ye who wait for the Lord."

ALEXANDER

Literal Meaning
"PROTECTING MEN" — Greek
Suggested Character Quality or Godly Characteristic
BRAVE PROTECTOR
Suggested Lifetime Scripture Verse — Psalm 31:24
"Be strong and let your heart take courage, all ye who wait for the Lord."

ALEXIS

Literal Meaning
PROTECTING MAN
Suggested Character Quality or Godly Characteristic
SECURE SPIRIT
Suggested Lifetime Scripture Verse — Psalm 32:7
"Thou art my hiding place; Thou wilt preserve me from trouble. Thou wilt surround me with songs of deliverance."

ALFRED

Literal Meaning
GOOD COUNSELOR
Suggested Character Quality or Godly Characteristic
A GOOD COUNSELOR
Suggested Lifetime Scripture Verse — Proverbs 20:5
"Planning in a man's mind is deep water, but a man of understanding will draw it out."

ALICE

Literal Meaning
TRUTHFUL ONE

Suggested Character Quality or Godly Characteristic
TRUTH
Suggested Lifetime Scripture Verse — Psalm 51:6
"Surely, Thou desirest truth in the inner self, and Thou makest me to understand hidden wisdom."

ALICIA

Literal Meaning
TRUTHFUL ONE
Suggested Character Quality or Godly Characteristic
TRUTHFUL ONE
Suggested Lifetime Scripture Verse — Psalm 51:6
"Surely, Thou desirest truth in the inner self, and Thou makest me to understand hidden wisdom."

ALLAN

Literal Meaning
HANDSOME, CHEERFUL, HARMONIOUS ONE
Suggested Character Quality or Godly Characteristic
CHEERFUL ONE
Suggested Lifetime Scripture Verse — Jeremiah 15:16
"Thy words were found, and I ate them, and Thy words were to me a joy and a rejoicing of my heart; for I bear Thy name, O Lord, God of hosts."

ALLISON

Literal Meaning
LITTLE TRUTHFUL ONE
Suggested Character Quality or Godly Characteristic
TRUTHFUL ONE
Suggested Lifetime Scripture Verse — Psalm 51:6
"Surely, Thou desirest truth in the inner self, and Thou makest me to understand hidden wisdom."

ALMA

Literal Meaning
LOVING, KIND
Suggested Character Quality or Godly Characteristic
LOVING AND KIND

A

Suggested Lifetime Scripture Verse — Psalm 5:7
"But as for me, by the greatness of Thy unfailing love I will enter Thy house; at Thy holy temple I will worship in reverence of Thee."

ALYCE

Literal Meaning
TRUTHFUL
Suggested Character Quality or Godly Characteristic
TRUTHFUL ONE
Suggested Lifetime Scripture Verse — Psalm 51:6
"Surely, Thou desirest truth in the inner self, and Thou makest me to understand hidden wisdom."

ALYSSA

Literal Meaning
TRUTH
Suggested Character Quality or Godly Characteristic
TRUTHFUL ONE
Suggested Lifetime Scripture Verse — Psalm 51:6
"Surely, Thou desirest truth in the inner self, and Thou makest me to understand hidden wisdom."

ALTA

Literal Meaning
HIGH OR LOFTY
Suggested Character Quality or Godly Characteristic
NOBLE SPIRIT
Suggested Lifetime Scripture Verse — Proverbs 2:6
"For the Lord gives wisdom; from His mouth come knowledge and discernment."

ALTON

Literal Meaning
DWELLER AT THE OLD TOWN OR ESTATE
Suggested Character Quality or Godly Characteristic
RESOURCEFUL
Suggested Lifetime Scripture Verse — Psalm 1:2
"But his delight is in the law of the Lord and His law he ponders day and night."

Explanation:
The character quality suggested is good citizenship, not only
in an earthly place but also in the heavenly kingdom.

ALVERA

Literal Meaning
EXCELLING
Suggested Character Quality or Godly Characteristic
EXCELLENT SPIRIT
Suggested Lifetime Scripture Verse — Psalm 86:12
*"I will praise Thee, O lord my God, with all my heart,
and I will glorify Thy name forever!"*

ALVIN

Literal Meaning
FRIEND OF ALL
Suggested Character Quality or Godly Characteristic
NOBLE FRIEND
Suggested Lifetime Scripture Verse — Psalm 112:4
*"Light rises for the upright in times of darkness; gracious
and merciful is the good man."*

AMANDA

Literal Meaning
WORTHY OF LOVE
Suggested Character Quality or Godly Characteristic
BELOVED
Suggested Lifetime Scripture Verse — I John 4:7
*"Beloved, let us love one another, because love springs from
God and whoever loves has been born of God and knows
God."*

AMBROSE

Literal Meaning
DIVINE, IMMORTAL ONE
Suggested Character Quality or Godly Characteristic
ENDURING
Suggested Lifetime Scripture Verse — James 1:12
"Blessed is the man who stands up under trial; for when

A

he has stood the test, he will receive the crown of life that God has promised to those who love Him."

AMOS

Literal Meaning
BEARER OF A BURDEN
Suggested Character Quality or Godly Characteristic
COMPASSIONATE SPIRIT
Suggested Lifetime Scripture Verse — Romans 12:9, 10
"*Let your love be sincere, clinging to the right with abhorrence of evil. Be joined together in a brotherhood of mutual love. . .*"

Explanation:
One who bears another's burden shows real love.

AMY

Literal Meaning
BELOVED ONE
Suggested Character Quality or Godly Characteristic
BELOVED
Suggested Lifetime Scripture Verse — I John 4:7
"*Beloved, let us love one another, because love springs from God and whoever loves has been born of God and knows God.*"

ANDREA

Literal Meaning
WOMANLY
Suggested Character Quality or Godly Characteristic
GODLY WOMAN
Suggested Lifetime Scripture Verse — Psalm 97:12
"*You who are righteous, rejoice in the Lord; be thankful for the consciousness of His holiness.*"

ANDREW

Literal Meaning
STRONG, MANLY
Suggested Character Quality or Godly Characteristic
STRONG, MANLY

Suggested Lifetime Scripture Verse — Daniel 2:23
"I thank Thee and praise Thee, O God of my fathers; for Thou has given me wisdom and strength."

ANGELA

Literal Meaning
ANGEL OR MESSENGER
Suggested Character Quality or Godly Characteristic
BRINGER OF TRUTH
Suggested Lifetime Scripture Verse — Psalm 89:1
"I will sing of the mercies of the Lord forever; I will make known Thy faithfulness with my mouth from generation to generation."

ANGUS

Literal Meaning
UNIQUE CHOICE
Suggested Character Quality or Godly Characteristic
CREATIVE SPIRIT
Suggested Lifetime Scripture Verse — Ephesians 2:10
"For we are His handiwork, created in Christ Jesus for good works, which God previously prepared for us so that we should live in them."

ANITA

Literal Meaning
GRACEFUL ONE
Suggested Character Quality or Godly Characteristic
GRACIOUS ONE
Suggested Lifetime Scripture Verse — Psalm 119:112
"I have set my heart on practicing Thy statutes forever, even to the end."

Explanation:
See Ann

ANN

Literal Meaning
GRACEFUL ONE

A

Suggested Character Quality or Godly Characteristic
GRACIOUS ONE
Suggested Lifetime Scripture Verse — Psalm 119:112
"I have set my heart on practicing Thy statutes forever, even to the end."

Explanation:
Graceful does not refer merely to physical ability, but to a quality of graciousness and mercy in the inner person.

ANNA

Literal Meaning
GRACEFUL ONE
Suggested Character Quality or Godly Characteristic
GRACIOUS ONE
Suggested Lifetime Scripture Verse — Psalm 119:112
"I have set my heart on practicing Thy statutes forever, even to the end."

Explanation:
See Ann

ANNE

Literal Meaning
GRACIOUS ONE
Suggested Character Quality or Godly Characteristic
GRACIOUS ONE
Suggested Lifetime Scripture Verse — Psalm 119:112
"I have set my heart on practicing Thy statutes forever, even to the end."

Explanation:
See Ann

ANNETTE

Literal Meaning
GRACEFUL ONE
Suggested Character Quality or Godly Characteristic
GRACIOUS ONE
Suggested Lifetime Scripture Verse — Psalm 119:112
"I have set my heart on practicing Thy statutes forever, even to the end."

Explanation:
See Ann

ANTHONY

Literal Meaning
INESTIMABLE
Suggested Character Quality or Godly Characteristic
PRICELESS ONE
Suggested Lifetime Scripture Verse — Psalm 21:6
"Yes, forever Thou dost make him most blessed; Thou dost delight him with joy by Thy presence."

APRIL

Literal Meaning
OPENING; BORN IN APRIL
Suggested Character Quality or Godly Characteristic
NEW IN FAITH
Suggested Lifetime Scripture Verse — Psalm 143:8
"In the morning proclaim to me Thy covenant love, for I have put my trust in Thee. Make me understand the way I should go, for I lift up my soul to Thee."

Explanation:
April suggests a time of freshness and beginnings, a time for new faith in God.

APRYL

Literal Meaning
OPENING; BORN IN APRIL
Suggested Character Quality or Godly Characteristic
NEW IN FAITH
Suggested Lifetime Scripture Verse — Psalm 143:8
"In the morning proclaim to me Thy covenant love, for I have put my trust in Thee. Make me understand the way I should go, for I lift up my soul to Thee."

Explanation:
See April

ARDELLE

Literal Meaning
WARMTH, ENTHUSIASM

A

Suggested Character Quality or Godly Characteristic
DEVOTED HEART
Suggested Lifetime Scripture Verse — Psalm 42:1
"As a deer pants for water brooks so my soul longs for Thee, O God."

ARDYCE

Literal Meaning
WARMTH, ENTHUSIASM
Suggested Character Quality or Godly Characteristic
ZEALOUS FOR GOD
Suggested Lifetime Scripture Verse — Colossians 3:23
"Whatever you do, work heartily as for the Lord and not for men."

ARLAND

Literal Meaning
PLEDGE
Suggested Character Quality or Godly Characteristic
DEPENDABLE ONE
Suggested Lifetime Scripture Verse — Psalm 5:8
"O Lord, lead me in Thy righteousness because of those who watch me; make Thy way straight before me."

ARLENE

Literal Meaning
A PLEDGE
Suggested Character Quality or Godly Characteristic
FAITHFUL ONE
Suggested Lifetime Scripture Verse — Psalm 34:1
"I will bless the Lord at all times; his praise shall continually be in my mouth."

ARNOLD

Literal Meaning
EAGLE RULER OR STRONG AS AN EAGLE
Suggested Character Quality or Godly Characteristic
BRAVE AND STRONG
Suggested Lifetime Scripture Verse — Isaiah 12:2

"Behold, God is my salvation; I will trust and not be afraid, for Jehovah, the Lord, is my strength and my song; yes, He has become my salvation."

ARON

Literal Meaning
LOFTY OR EXALTED
Suggested Character Quality or Godly Characteristic
EXALTED
Suggested Lifetime Scripture Verse — Psalm 3:3
"But thou, O Lord, art a shield about me; my glory and the One who lifts my head."

ARTHUR

Literal Meaning
NOBLE ONE OR BEAR MAN
Suggested Character Quality or Godly Characteristic
MAN OF INTEGRITY
Suggested Lifetime Scripture Verse — Psalm 37:23
"A person's steps are confirmed by the Lord; He establishes him and delights in his way."

AUDREY

Literal Meaning
NOBLE STRENGTH
Suggested Character Quality or Godly Characteristic
NOBLE AND STRONG
Suggested Lifetime Scripture Verse — Psalm 138:3
"In the day when I called Thou didst answer me, and didst encourage me with strength in my soul."

AUSTIN

Literal Meaning
WORTHY OF REVERENCE
Suggested Character Quality or Godly Characteristic
NOBLE HEART
Suggested Lifetime Scripture Verse — Psalm 119:58
"Wholeheartedly I sought Thy favor; be merciful to me according to Thy word."

A

AVERY

Literal Meaning
SELF-COUNSEL
Suggested Character Quality or Godly Characteristic
A GOOD COUNSELOR
Suggested Lifetime Scripture Verse — Proverbs 20:5
"Planning in a man's mind is deep water, but a man of understanding will draw it out."

AVON

Literal Meaning:
None Could Be Found
Suggested Character Quality or Godly Characteristic
GENEROUS ONE
Suggested Lifetime Scripture Verse — Psalm 54:6
"With a freewill offering I will sacrifice to Thee; I will praise Thy name, O Lord, for it is good."

Explanation:
No literal meaning could be found for this name. The character quality selected suggests service both to God and man.

BARBARA

Literal Meaning
STRANGER
Suggested Character Quality or Godly Characteristic
COMING WITH JOY
Suggested Lifetime Scripture Verse — I Thessalonians 3:12
"*May the Lord make your love for one another and for everyone abundant and running over, just as ours is for you.*"

Explanation:
A stranger comes into new surroundings with a certain attitude; one who is in the Lord comes with joy and love.

BARBIE

Literal Meaning
STRANGER
Suggested Character Quality or Godly Characteristic
COMING WITH JOY
Suggested Lifetime Scripture Verse — I Thessalonians 3:12
"*May the Lord make your love for one another and for everyone abundant and running over, just as ours is for you.*"

Explanation:
See Barbara

BARNABY

Literal Meaning
SON OF PROPHECY
Suggested Character Quality or Godly Characteristic
REVERENT SPIRIT

B

Suggested Lifetime Scripture Verse — Hebrews 12:28
"*Let us, therefore, be grateful that the kingdom we have received cannot be shaken, and so let us serve God acceptably with reverence and awe.*"

BARRY

Literal Meaning
SPEARLIKE OR POINTED
Suggested Character Quality or Godly Characteristic
COURAGEOUS
Suggested Lifetime Scripture Verse — Psalm 18:30
"*God! Perfect is His way! The word of the Lord is proven; a shield is He to all who trust in Him.*"

Explanation:
Where warlike or soldierly meanings occur, qualities necessary for those in combat are selected.

BART

Literal Meaning
SON OF THE FURROWS; FARMER
Suggested Character Quality or Godly Characteristic
DILIGENT ONE
Suggested Lifetime Scripture Verse — Psalm 37:3
"*Trust in the Lord and do good; inhabit the land and practice faithfulness.*"

BASIL

Literaly Meaning
KINGLY
Suggested Character Quality or Godly Characteristic
GRACIOUS AND MANLY
Suggested Lifetime Scripture Verse — Psalm 112:6, 7
"*Such a man will never be laid low, for the just shall be held in remembrance forever. He need never fear any evil report; his heart will remain firm, fully trusting in the Lord.*"

BEATA

Literal Meaning
BLESSED, HAPPY ONE

Suggested Character Quality or Godly Characteristic
BRINGER OF JOY
Suggested Lifetime Scripture Verse — John 15:11
"I have talked these matters over with you so that my joy may be in you and your joy be made complete."

BEATRICE

Literal Meaning
SHE WHO MAKES OTHERS HAPPY
Suggested Character Quality or Godly Characteristic
BRINGER OF JOY
Suggested Lifetime Scripture Verse — Isaiah 30:29
"But you shall have a song as in the night consecrated for a feasting; and you shall have the gladness of heart as when men march with flutes to come to the mountain of the Lord, the Rock of Israel."

BELVA

Literal Meaning
BEAUTIFUL ONE
Suggested Character Quality or Godly Characteristic
INNER BEAUTY
Suggested Lifetime Scripture Verse — Hebrews 12:28
"Let us, therefore, be grateful that the kingdom we have received cannot be shaken, and so let us serve God acceptably with reverence and awe."

BEN

Literal Meaning
SON OF THE RIGHT HAND
Suggested Character Quality or Godly Characteristic
FAVORED SON
Suggested Lifetime Scripture Verse — Psalm 40:11
"Thou, O Lord, wilt not withhold Thy mercies from me; Thy lovingkindness and Thy truth shall continually preserve me."

BENEDICT

Literal Meaning
SPOKEN WELL OF, BLESSED

B

Suggested Character Quality or Godly Characteristic
BLESSED BY GOD
Suggested Lifetime Scripture Verse — Psalm 119:2
"Blessed are those who keep His testimonies, who seek Him wholeheartedly."

BENJAMIN

Literal Meaning
SON OF THE RIGHT HAND
Suggested Character Quality or Godly Characteristic
FAVORED SON
Suggested Lifetime Scripture Verse — Psalm 40:11
"Thou, O Lord, wilt not withhold Thy mercies from me; Thy lovingkindness and Thy truth shall continually preserve me."

BERNADETTE

Literal Meaning
BRAVE AS A BEAR
Suggested Character Quality or Godly Characteristic
STRONG; WOMANLY
Suggested Lifetime Scripture Verse — Psalm 18:32
"The God who girds me with strength, and makes my way perfect."

BERNARD

Literal Meaning
BRAVE AS A BEAR
Suggested Character Quality or Godly Characteristic
MIGHTY, POWERFUL
Suggested Lifetime Scripture Verse — Colossians 4:2
"Keep persevering in prayer; attend to it diligently with the offering of thanks."

BERNICE

Literal Meaning
HARBINGER OF VICTORY
Suggested Character Quality or Godly Characteristic
VICTORIOUS

Suggested Lifetime Scripture Verse — Isaiah 48:17
*"Thus says the Lord, your Redeemer, the Holy One of Israel:
I am the Lord your God, who teaches you to profit, who
leads you in the way you should go."*

BERNITA

Literal Meaning
HARBINGER OF VICTORY
Suggested Character Quality or Godly Characteristic
VICTORIOUS
Suggested Lifetime Scripture Verse — Isaiah 48:17
*"Thus says the Lord, your Redeemer, the Holy One of Israel:
I am the Lord your God, who teaches you to profit, who leads
you in the way you should go."*

BERT

Literal Meaning
SHINING, GLORIOUS ONE
Suggested Character Quality or Godly Characteristic
MAN OF HONOR
Suggested Lifetime Scripture Verse — Isaiah 30:18
*"Nevertheless the Lord longs to be gracious to you! Therefore
He shall rise up to bestow mercy on you; for the Lord is
a God of justice. Blessed are they who wait for Him."*

BERTHA

Literal Meaning
"BRIGHT" — Germanic
Suggested Character Quality or Godly Characteristic
BRIGHT ONE
Suggested Lifetime Scripture Verse — Psalm 97:11
*"Light is sown for the righteous and joy for those whose
hearts are right."*

BERTRAM

Literal Meaning
ILLUSTRIOUS
Suggested Character Quality or Godly Characteristic
MAN OF HONOR

B

Suggested Lifetime Scripture Verse — Isaiah 30:18
"Nevertheless the Lord longs to be gracious to you! Therefore He shall rise up to bestow mercy on you; for the Lord is a God of justice. Blessed are they who wait for Him."

BESSIE

Literal Meaning
CONSECRATED TO GOD
Suggested Character Quality or Godly Characteristic
CONSECRATED TO GOD
Suggested Lifetime Scripture Verse — Psalm 119:34
"Give me understanding, and I shall observe Thy law, and keep it wholeheartedly."

Explanation:
See Elizabeth

BETH

Literal Meaning
HOUSE OF GOD
Suggested Character Quality or Godly Characteristic
ABIDING PLACE OF GOD
Suggested Lifetime Scripture Verse — Psalm 23:6
"Surely, goodness and unfailing love shall follow me all the days of my life and I shall dwell in the house of the Lord forever."

BETSY

Literal Meaning
No Literal Meaning found
Suggested Character Quality or Godly Characteristic
CONSECRATED TO GOD
Suggested Lifetime Scripture Verse — Psalm 119:34
"Give me understanding, and I shall observe Thy law, and keep it wholeheartedly."

Explanation:
See Elizabeth

BETTY

Literal Meaning
No literal meaning found
Suggested Character Quality or Godly Characteristic
CONSECRATED TO GOD
Suggested Lifetime Scripture Verse — Psalm 116:13
"*I will take the cup of salvation and call on the name of the Lord.*"

Explanation:
See Elizabeth

BEVERLY

Literal Meaning
DWELLER AT THE BEAVER MEADOW
Suggested Character Quality or Godly Characteristic
DILIGENT SPIRIT
Suggested Lifetime Scripture Verse — Colossians 3:23
"*Whatever you do, work heartily as for the Lord and not for men.*"

BILL

Literal Meaning
RESOLUTE PROTECTOR
Suggested Character Quality or Godly Characteristic
GREAT PROTECTOR
Suggested Lifetime Scripture Verse — Micah 6:8
"*And what does the Lord require of you but to do justice, to love mercy and to walk humbly with your God.*"

BLANCHE

Literal Meaning
WHITE FAIR ONE
Suggested Character Quality or Godly Characteristic
PURITY
Suggested Lifetime Scripture Verse — Proverbs 31:30
"*Charm is deceitful and beauty is passing, but a woman who reveres the Lord will be praised.*"

B

BOB

Literal Meaning
BRIGHT OR SHINING WITH FAME
Suggested Character Quality or Godly Characteristic
EXCELLENT WORTH
Suggested Lifetime Scripture Verse — Psalm 24:3-4
"Who shall go up into the mountain of the Lord; who shall stand in His holy place? He who has clean hands and a pure heart, who has not lifted up his soul to falsehood, who has not sworn deceptively."

BOBBI

Literal Meaning
SHINING WITH FAME
Suggested Character Quality or Godly Characteristic
EXCELLENT WORTH
Suggested Lifetime Scripture Verse — Philippians 4:13
"I have strength for every situation through Him who empowers me."

BOBBY

Literal Meaning
BRIGHT OR SHINING WITH FAME
Suggested Character Quality or Godly Characteristic
EXCELLENT WORTH
Suggested Lifetime Scripture Verse — Psalm 24:3-4
"Who shall go up into the mountain of the Lord; who shall stand in His holy place? He who has clean hands and a pure heart, who has not lifted up his soul to falsehood, who has not sworn deceptively."

BONNIE

Literal Meaning
SWEET AND GOOD
Suggested Character Quality or Godly Characteristic
A GOOD HEART
Suggested Lifetime Scripture Verse — Psalm 64:10
"The righteous shall be glad in the Lord, and trust in Him; and all the upright in heart shall offer praise."

BORIS

Literal Meaning
WARRIOR
Suggested Character Quality or Godly Characteristic
LOYAL HEART
Suggested Lifetime Scripture Verse — Deuteronomy 11:1
"Love the Lord your God, therefore, and always heed His charge, His laws, His ordinances, and His commandments. Of the Lord your God's discipline you must be ever mindful."

BRAD

Literal Meaning
FROM THE BROAD MEADOW
Suggested Character Quality or Godly Characteristic
ABUNDANT PROVIDER
Suggested Lifetime Scripture Verse — Psalm 1, 2
"The Lord is my Shepherd; I shall not lack; He makes me to lie down in green pastures."

Explanation:
A meadow suggests prosperity, peacefulness, security; the person who provides these things for others provides abundantly.

BRADLEY

Literal Meaning
FROM THE BROAD MEADOW
Suggested Character Quality or Godly Characteristic
ABUNDANT PROVIDER
Suggested Lifetime Scripture Verse — Psalm 23:1, 2
"The Lord is my Shepherd; I shall not lack; He makes me to lie down in green pastures."

Explanation:
See Brad

BRANDON

Literal Meaning
FROM THE BEACON HILL
Suggested Character Quality or Godly Characteristic
STRONG IN VICTORY

B

Suggested Lifetime Scripture Verse — Jeremiah 15:20
"And I will make you to this people a fortified wall of bronze. They will fight against you, but they shall not prevail over you; for I am with you to save you and to deliver you, says the Lord."

Explanation:
The beacon, a shining bright light, was used to signal victory from one camp to another.

BRANT

Literal Meaning
PROUD ONE
Suggested Character Quality or Godly Characteristic
RISING ABOVE
Suggested Lifetime Scripture Verse — Psalm 24:3-4
"Who shall go up into the mountain of the Lord; who shall stand in His holy place? He who has clean hands and a pure heart, who has not lifted up his soul to falsehood, who has not sworn deceptively."

BRENDA

Literal Meaning
FIERY
Suggested Character Quality or Godly Characteristic
ENTHUSIASTIC
Suggested Lifetime Scripture Verse — Psalm 119:16
"I take great delight in Thy statutes; and I will not forget Thy word."

BRENDON

Literal Meaning
FROM THE FIERY HILL
Suggested Character Quality or Godly Characteristic
STRONG IN VICTORY
Suggested Lifetime Scripture Verse — Jeremiah 15:20
"And I will make you to this people a fortified wall of bronze. They will fight against you, but they shall not prevail over you; for I am with you to save you and to deliver you, says the Lord."

BRENT

Literal Meaning
STEEP HILL
Suggested Character Quality or Godly Characteristic
RISING ABOVE
Suggested Lifetime Scripture Verse — Psalm 24:3-4
"Who shall go up into the mountain of the Lord; who shall stand in His holy place? He who has clean hands and a pure heart, who has not lifted up his soul to falsehood, who has not sworn deceptively."

BRIAN

Literal Meaning
STRENGTH, VIRTURE, HONOR
Suggested Character Quality or Godly Characteristic
STRONG IN VIRTUE
Suggested Lifetime Scripture Verse — Proverbs 24:5
"A wise man is strong, and a man of knowledge adds to his strength."

BRICE

Literal Meaning
QUICK ONE
Suggested Character Quality or Godly Characteristic
QUICK TO EXCEL
Suggested Lifetime Scripture Verse — Psalm 5:12
"Thou, O Lord, dost bless the righteous; as with a shield Thou dost surround him with favor."

BRUCE

Literal Meaning
DWELLER AT THE THICKET
Suggested Character Quality or Godly Characteristic
SECURE ONE
Suggested Lifetime Scripture Verse — Romans 8:2
"For the life-giving principles of the Spirit have freed you in Christ Jesus from the control of the principles of sin and death."

B

Explanation:
A thicket was often used to protect land and crops; therefore one who lived there would be secure.

BRYAN

Literal Meaning
STRENGTH, VIRTUE, HONOR
Suggested Character Quality or Godly Characteristic
STRONG IN SPIRIT
Suggested Lifetime Scripture Verse — Psalm 31:3
"For Thou art my rock and my fortress; for Thy name's sake lead me and guide me."

BRYCE

Literal Meaning
QUICK ONE
Suggested Character Quality or Godly Characteristic
QUICK TO EXCEL
Suggested Lifetime Scripture Verse — Psalm 5:12
"Thou, O Lord, dost bless the righteous; as with a shield Thou dost surround him with favor."

BURT

Literal Meaning
BRIGHT; OR BOROUGH TOWN
Suggested Character Quality or Godly Characteristic
ABUNDANT PROVIDER
Suggested Lifetime Scripture Verse — Psalm 23:1, 2
"The Lord is my Shepherd; I shall not lack; He makes me to lie down in green pastures."

BYRON

Literal Meaning
"BEAR" — Anglo-Saxon
Suggested Character Quality or Godly Characteristic
FULL OF STRENGTH
Suggested Lifetime Scripture Verse — Psalm 59:9
"O my Strength, I will wait on Thee, for God is my stronghold."

Explanation:
"Bear" suggests physical, emotional and mental strength.

CALVIN

Literal Meaning
BALD ONE
Suggested Character Quality or Godly Characteristic
HUMBLE
Suggested Lifetime Scripture Verse — Proverbs 22:4
"The results of humility—reverence for the Lord—are riches, honor and life."

Explanation:
The Lord often used baldness to motivate one to humility; therefore the character quality "humble" is appropriate.

CANDICE

Literal Meaning
GLITTERING, GLOWING WHITE
Suggested Character Quality or Godly Characteristic
WOMAN OF HONOR
Suggested Lifetime Scripture Verse — Habakkuk 3:19
"The Lord God is my strength; He makes my feet like hinds' feet, He makes me tread upon my high places."

CARL

Literal Meaning
FARMER
Suggested Character Quality or Godly Characteristic
STRONG; MANLY
Suggested Lifetime Scripture Verse — Ephesians 6:10
"In conclusion, be strong in the Lord and in the strength of His might."

C

CARLA

Litteral Meaning
LITTLE WOMANLY ONE
Suggested Character Quality or Godly Characteristic
STRONG; WOMANLY
Suggested Lifetime Scripture Verse — Isaiah 41:10
"Fear not, for I am with you; be not dismayed, for I am your God! I will strengthen you; yes, I will help you; yes, I will uphold you with My vindicating right hand."

CARMEN

Literal Meaning
SONG
Suggested Character Quality or Godly Characteristic
SONG OF JOY
Suggested Lifetime Scripture Verse — Psalm 116:17
"I will offer to Thee the sacrifice of thanksgiving and call on the name of the Lord."

CARMINE

Literal Meaning
A SONG
Suggested Character Quality or Godly Characteristic
LIVING IN HARMONY
Suggested Lifetime Scripture Verse — Psalm 42:11
"Why are you bowed down, O my soul, and why do you groan within me? Hope in God, for I shall yet praise Him, my face-healer and my God."

CAROL

Literal Meaning
WOMANLY; SONG
Suggested Character Quality or Godly Characteristic
SONG OF JOY
Suggested Lifetime Scripture Verse — John 15:11
"I have talked these matters over with you so that my joy may be in you and your joy be made complete."

CAROLINE

Literal Meaning
LITTLE, WOMANLY ONE
Suggested Character Quality or Godly Characteristic
REFRESHING JOY
Suggested Lifetime Scripture Verse — Psalm 119:16
"*I take great delight in Thy statutes; I will not forget Thy word.*"

CAROLYN

Literal Meaning
LITTLE WOMANLY ONE; SONG
Suggested Character Quality or Godly Characteristic
JOYFUL SPIRIT
Suggested Lifetime Scripture Verse — Jeremiah 33:11
"*The voice of joy and the voice of gladness, the voice of the bridegroom and the voice of the bride, and the voices of those who say, 'Give thanks to the Lord of hosts, for the Lord is good, for His mercy endures forever,' and who bring sacrifices of thanksgiving to the house of the Lord. For I will restore the fortunes of the land as formerly, says the Lord.*"

CARRIE

Literal Meaning
STRONG; WOMANLY
Suggested Character Quality or Godly Characteristic
STRONG WOMAN
Suggested Lifetime Scripture Verse — Isaiah 41:10
"*Fear not, for I am with you; be not dismayed, for I am your God! I will strengthen you; yes, I will help you; yes, I will uphold you with My vindicating right hand.*"

CARTER

Literal Meaning
MAKER OF CARTS
Suggested Character Quality or Godly Characteristic
INDUSTRIOUS SPIRIT

C

Suggested Lifetime Scripture Verse — Hebrews 13:16
"*Do not forget to do good and be generous, for with such sacrifices God is well pleased.*"

CATHERINE

Literal Meaning
PURE ONE
Suggested Character Quality or Godly Characteristic
PURE ONE
Suggested Lifetime Scripture Verse — Psalm 119:7
"*I will give thanks to Thee with integrity of heart when I learn Thy righteous judgments.*"

CATHLEEN

Literal Meaning
PURE
Suggested Character Quality or Godly Characteristic
PURE ONE
Suggested Lifetime Scripture Verse — Psalm 119:7
"*I will praise Thee with an upright heart, when I learn Thy righteous ordinances.*"

CATHY

Literal Meaning
PURE
Suggested Character Quality or Godly Characteristic
PURE ONE
Suggested Lifetime Scripture Verse — Psalm 119:7
"*I will praise Thee with an upright heart, when I learn Thy righteous ordinances.*"

CECIL

Literal Meaning
BLIND
Suggested Character Quality or Godly Characteristic
HUMBLE SPIRIT
Suggested Lifetime Scripture Verse — Psalm 10:17
"*Lord, Thou hast heard the desire of the humble: Thou wilt prepare their heart. Thou wilt cause thine ear to hear.*"

Explanation:
See Cecilia

CECILIA

Literal Meaning
BLIND
Suggested Character Quality or Godly Characteristic
HUMBLE SPIRIT
Suggested Lifetime Scripture Verse — Psalm 10:17
"Lord, Thou hast heard the desire of the humble: Thou wilt prepare their heart, Thou wilt cause Thine ear to hear."

Explanation:
Acceptance of one's condition is the first step is humility; the blind must learn this before they can be helped.

CHAD

Literal Meaning
WARLIKE
Suggested Character Quality or Godly Characteristic
DEFENDER
Suggested Lifetime Scripture Verse — Isaiah 1:17
"Learn to do good! Seek justice; restrain the ruthless; protect the orphan; defend the widow."

CHARLENE

Literal Meaning
LITTLE WOMANLY ONE
Suggested Character Quality or Godly Characteristic
WOMANLY
Suggested Lifetime Scripture Verse — Proverbs 31:10
"Who can find a wife with strength of character? She is far more precious than jewels."

CHARLES

Literal Meaning
STRONG; MANLY
Suggested Character Quality or Godly Characteristic
STRONG; MANLY
Suggested Lifetime Scripture Verse — Joshua 1:9
"Have I not commanded you? Be resolute and strong! Be

C

not afraid, and be not dismayed; for the Lord your God is with you everywhere you go."

CHARLOTTE

Literal Meaning
LITTLE WOMANLY ONE
Suggested Character Quality or Godly Characteristic
FULL OF GRACE
Suggested Lifetime Scripture Verse — Psalm 23:6
"Surely goodness and unfailing love shall follow me all the days of my life and I shall dwell in the house of the Lord forever."

CHERI

Literal Meaning
DEAR BELOVED ONE
Suggested Character Quality or Godly Characteristic
CHERISHED ONE
Suggested Lifetime Scripture Verse — Zephaniah 3:17
"The Lord, your God, is in your midst, a mighty one who will save. He will rejoice over you with delight; He will rest you in His love; He will be joyful over you with singing."

CHERISE

Literal Meaning
DEAR BELOVED ONE
Suggested Character Quality or Godly Characteristic
CHERISHED ONE
Suggested Lifetime Scripture Verse — Zephaniah 3:17
"The Lord, your God, is in your midst, a mighty one who will save. He will rejoice over you with delight; He will rest you in His love; He will be joyful over you with singing."

CHERYL

Literal Meaning
THE EPITOME OF FEMININITY
Suggested Character Quality or Godly Characteristic
WOMANLY

Suggested Lifetime Scripture Verse — Proverbs 31:10
"Who can find a virtuous woman? for her price is far above rubies."

CHESTER

Literal Meaning
DWELLER AT THE FORTIFIED ARMY CAMP
Suggested Character Quality or Godly Characteristic
STRONG DEFENDER
Suggested Lifetime Scripture Verse — Psalm 31:3
"For Thou art my rock and my fortress; for Thy name's sake lead me and guide me."

CHRISTIAN

Literal Meaning
BELIEVER IN CHRIST
Suggested Character Quality or Godly Characteristic
FOLLOWER OF CHRIST
Suggested Lifetime Scripture Verse — Psalm 86:11
"Teach me Thy way, O Lord; I will walk in Thy truth; unite my heart to revere Thy name."

CHRISTINE

Literal Meaning
CHRISTIAN
Suggested Character Quality or Godly Characteristic
FOLLOWER OF CHRIST
Suggested Lifetime Scripture Verse — Psalm 63:8
"My soul follows close behind Thee; Thy right hand upholds me."

CHRISTOPHER

Literal Meaning
CHRIST-BEARER
Suggested Character Quality or Godly Characteristic
FOLLOWER OF CHRIST
Suggested Lifetime Scripture Verse — Psalm 86:11
"Teach me Thy way, O Lord; I will walk in Thy truth; unite my heart to revere Thy name."

C

CHUCK

Literal Meaning
STRONG; MANLY
Suggested Character Quality or Godly Characteristic
FEARLESS, STRONG
Suggested Lifetime Scripture Verse — Proverbs 28:1, 12
"The wicked flee when there is one pursuing, but the righteous are as fearless as a young lion ... When the righteous rejoice, great is the glory; but when the wicked rise, men hide themselves."

CINDY

Literal Meaning
GODDESS OF THE MOON
Suggested Character Quality or Godly Characteristic
REFLECTOR OF LIGHT
Suggested Lifetime Scripture Verse — Psalm 27:1
"The Lord is my light and my salvation; whom shall I fear? The Lord is the stronghold of my life; of whom shall I be afraid?"

Explanation:
The moon reflects the light of the sun; we are to reflect God's Son.

CLARA

Literal Meaning
BRILLIANT, BRIGHT, ILLUSTRIOUS
Suggested Character Quality or Godly Characteristic
PURE IN GRACE
Suggested Lifetime Scripture Verse — II Timothy 2:22
"But flee from the lusts of youth. Go in pursuit of integrity, faith, love, peace, in fellowship with those who call upon the Lord out of pure hearts."

CLARENCE

Literal Meaning
FAMOUS ONE
Suggested Character Quality or Godly Characteristic
STRONG IN CHARACTER

Suggested Lifetime Scripture Verse — Philippians 1:6
"Of this I am convinced, that He who has begun a good work in you will bring it to completion in the day of Christ Jesus."

CLARK

Literal Meaning
"LEARNED" — Latin
Suggested Character Quality or Godly Characteristic
FULL OF WISDOM
Suggested Lifetime Scripture Verse — Psalm 49:3
"My mouth shall speak wisdom; and the thoughts of my heart shall be of insight."

CLAUDE

Literal Meaning
"LAME" — Latin
Suggested Character Quality or Godly Characteristic
OF HUMBLE HEART
Suggested Lifetime Scripture Verse — Psalm 54:4
"Behold, God is my ally; the Lord is with those who sustain my soul."

Explanation:
"Lame" suggests dependence. The humble person recognizes weakness and accepts it.

CLAUDETTE

Literal Meaning
LAME
Suggested Character Quality or Godly Characteristic
FULL OF HUMILITY
Suggested Lifetime Scripture Verse — Psalm 5:8
"O Lord, lead me in Thy righteousness because of those who watch me; make Thy way straight before me."

CLAUDIA

Literal Meaning
LAME ONE

C

Suggested Character Quality or Godly Characteristic
OF HUMBLE HEART
Suggested Lifetime Scripture Verse — Isaiah 30:15
"*For thus says the Lord God, The Holy One of Israel: In conversion and rest you shall be saved; in quietness and confidence shall be your strength.*"

Explanation:
All inabilities provide opportunities for God's power.

CLAUDINE

Literal Meaning
THE LAME ONE
Suggested Character Quality or Godly Characteristic
HUMILITY OF SPIRIT
Suggested Lifetime Scripture Verse — Isaiah 30:15
"*For thus says the Lord God, The Holy One of Israel: In conversion and rest you shall be saved; in quietness and confidence shall be your strength.*"

Explanation:
See Claudia

CLAY

Literal Meaning
TOWN AT A CLAY SITE
Suggested Character Quality or Godly Characteristic
IN GOD'S MOLD
Suggested Lifetime Scripture Verse — Jeremiah 18:6
"*O house of Israel, cannot I do with you as this potter did? says the Lord. Take notice, just as the clay is in the potter's hand, so are you in My hand, O house of Israel.*"

CLAYTON

Literal Meaning
FROM THE CLAY ESTATE OR TOWN
Suggested Character Quality or Godly Characteristic
IN GOD'S MOLD
Suggested Lifetime Scripture Verse — Jeremiah 18:6
"*O house of Israel, cannot I do with you as this potter did? says the Lord. Take notice, just as the clay is in the potter's hand, so are you in My hand, O house of Israel.*"

CLIFF

Literal Meaning
TOWN AT A CLIFF
Suggested Character Quality or Godly Characteristic
VIGILANT
Suggested Lifetime Scripture Verse — I Corinthians 16:13
"Be alert; stand firm in the faith; play the man; be strong."

CLIFFORD

Literal Meaning
FROM THE CLIFF-FORD
Suggested Character Quality or Godly Characteristic
VIGILANT
Suggested Lifetime Scripture Verse — I Corinthians 16:13
"Be alert; stand firm in the faith; play the man; be strong."

Explanation:
Many times a watchman was stationed at the fording place
in order to give advance warning of approaching enemies.

CLINT

Literal Meaning
FROM THE HEADLAND-ESTATE OR TOWN
Suggested Character Quality or Godly Characteristic
GREAT IN FORGIVENESS
Suggested Lifetime Scripture Verse — Amos 5:24
*"Let justice roll on like water, and righteousness like a
mighty stream."*

Explanation:
Arbitrarily chosen

CLYDE

Literal Meaning
HEARD FROM FAR AWAY
Suggested Character Quality or Godly Characteristic
OF GOOD REPORT
Suggested Lifetime Scripture Verse — Psalm 112:7
*"He need never fear any evil report; his heart will remain
firm, fully trusting in the Lord."*

C

COLETTE

Literal Meaning
VICTORIOUS ARMY
Suggested Character Quality or Godly Characteristic
VICTORIOUS SPIRIT
Suggested Lifetime Scripture Verse — I Corinthians 15:57
"But thanks be to God, who gives us the victory through our Lord Jesus Christ!"

COLLEEN

Literal Meaning
GIRL, MAIDEN
Suggested Character Quality or Godly Characteristic
VIRTUOUS SPIRIT
Suggested Lifetime Scripture Verse — Proverbs 2:11, 12
"Discretion will protect you; discernment will guard you, to deliver you from the way of evil, from men speaking perverted things."

CONNIE

Literal Meaning
FIRMNESS; CONSTANCY
Suggested Character Quality or Godly Characteristic
EARNEST DEVOTEE
Suggested Lifetime Scripture Verse — Psalm 34:1
"I will bless the Lord at all times; His praise shall continually be in my mouth."

CONRAD

Literal Meaning
ABLE IN COUNSEL
Suggested Character Quality or Godly Characteristic
FULL OF WISDOM
Suggested Lifetime Scripture Verse — Psalm 111:10
"For reverence of the Lord is the beginning of wisdom. There is insight in all who observe it. His praise is everlasting."

CONSTANCE

Literal Meaning
FIRMNESS; CONSTANCY

Suggested Character Quality or Godly Characteristic
DEVOTED SPIRIT
Suggested Lifetime Scripture Verse — Psalm 34:1
"*I will bless the Lord at all times; His praise shall continually be in my mouth.*"

CORA

Literal Meaning
"MAIDEN" — Greek
Suggested Character Quality or Godly Characteristic
VIRTUOUS HEART
Suggested Lifetime Scripture Verse — Psalm 31:5
"*Into Thy hand I commit my spirit; Thou hast redeemed me, Lord God of truth.*"

COREY

Literal Meaning
DWELLER BY A HOLLOW OR BY A SEETHING POOL
Suggested Character Quality or Godly Characteristic
PROSPEROUS ONE
Suggested Lifetime Scripture Verse — Psalm 13:6
"*Let me sing to the Lord because He has dealt generously with me.*"

CORNELIUS

Literal Meaning
"BATTLE HORN" — Latin
Suggested Character Quality or Godly Characteristic
VIGILANT SPIRIT
Suggested Lifetime Scripture Verse — Romans 12:12
"*Joyfully hoping as you endure affliction, persistent in prayer.*"

Explanation:
"Battle Horn" suggests the need for constant vigilance to give the right signal in battle.

COURTNEY

Literal Meaning
SHORT NOSE

C

Suggested Character Quality or Godly Characteristic
MAN OF DISCRETION
Suggested Lifetime Scripture Verse — Zechariah 7:9
"Thus says the Lord of hosts: Render true judgment; let every one show loving-kindness and compassion to his brother."

Explanation:
Someone with a short nose would not be sticking it in other people's business; therefore, discretion is an appropriate characteristic.

CRAIG

Literal Meaning
DWELLER AT THE CRAG
Suggested Character Quality or Godly Characteristic
STRONG; ENDURING
Suggested Lifetime Scripture Verse — Proverbs 24:5
"A wise man is strong, and a man of knowledge adds to his strength."

CURTIS

Literal Meaning
COURTEOUS ONE
Suggested Character Quality or Godly Characteristic
COURTEOUS ONE
Suggested Lifetime Scripture Verse — Zechariah 7:9
"Thus says the Lord of hosts: Render true judgment; let every one show loving-kindness and compassion to his brother."

CYNTHIA

Literal Meaning
THE MOON
Suggested Character Quality or Godly Characteristic
REFLECTOR OF LIGHT
Suggested Lifetime Scripture Verse — Psalm 27:1
"The Lord is my light and my salvation; whom shall I fear?"

Explanation:
See Cindy

CYRUS

Literal Meaning
THRONE; SUN
Suggested Character Quality or Godly Characteristic
OF GOOD CHARACTER
Suggested Lifetime Scripture Verse — Psalm 119:101
"I have refrained my feet from every evil way, that I might observe Thy word."

D

DALE

Literal Meaning
DWELLER IN THE VALLEY
Suggested Character Quality or Godly Characteristic
COURAGEOUS
Suggested Lifetime Scripture Verse — Psalm 23:4
"Yes, though I walk through the valley of the shadow of death, I will fear no harm; for Thou art with me: Thy rod and Thy staff, they comfort me."

DANA

Literal Meaning
A DANE
Suggested Character Quality or Godly Characteristic
INDUSTRIOUS SPIRIT
Suggested Lifetime Scripture Verse — Romans 12:11
"Never slacking in interest, serving the Lord, keeping spiritually aglow."

Explanation:
The people of the Scandinavian countries are known for their hard work and diligence.

DANIEL

Literal Meaning
GOD IS MY JUDGE
Suggested Character Quality or Godly Characteristic
GOD IS JUDGE
Suggested Lifetime Scripture Verse — Psalm 7:10
"My shield depends upon God, who saves the upright in heart."

DANNY

Literal Meaning
GOD IS MY JUDGE
Suggested Character Quality or Godly Characteristic
GOD IS JUDGE
Suggested Lifetime Scripture Verse — Psalm 7:10
"*My shield depends upon God, who saves the upright in heart.*"

DARLA

Literal Meaning
LITTLE DEAR ONE
Suggested Character Quality or Godly Characteristic
TENDERLY LOVED
Suggested Lifetime Scripture Verse — Song of Solomon 2:4
"*He has brought me into the banqueting hall, and His banner over me is love.*"

DARLENE

Literal Meaning
LITTLE DEAR ONE
Sugggested Character Quality or Godly Characteristic
TENDERLY LOVED
Suggested Lifetime Scripture Verse — Song of Solomon 2:4
"*He has brought me into the banqueting hall, and His banner over me is love.*"

DARREN

Literal Meaning
LITTLE GREAT ONE
Suggested Character Quality or Godly Characteristic
BLESSED WITH BOUNTY
Suggested Lifetime Scripture Verse — Proverbs 10:22
"*It is the blessing of the Lord that brings riches and toiling will add nothing to it.*"

DARRYL

Literal Meaning
BELOVED ONE

D

Suggested Character Quality or Godly Characteristic
BELOVED
Suggested Lifetime Scripture Verse — Psalm 32:10-11
"*Many sorrows are to the ungodly, but he who trusts in the Lord shall be encircled with lovingkindness. Be glad in the Lord and exult, ye righteous; shout joyfully, ye upright in heart.*"

DAVID

Literal Meaning
BELOVED ONE
Suggested Character Quality or Godly Characteristic
BELOVED
Suggested Lifetime Scripture Verse — I John 4:7
"*Beloved, let us love one another, because love springs from God and whoever loves has been born of God and knows God.*"

DAWN

Literal Meaning
THE DAWN OF DAY
Suggested Character Quality or Godly Characteristic
JOY AND PRAISE
Suggested Lifetime Scripture Verse — Psalm 143:8
"*In the morning proclaim to me Thy covenant love, for I have put my trust in Thee. Make me understand the way I should go, for I lift up my soul to Thee.*"

DEAN

Literal Meaning
DWELLER IN THE VALLEY
Suggested Character Quality or Godly Characteristic
COURAGEOUS HEART
Suggested Lifetime Scripture Verse — Psalm 16:8
"*I have placed the Lord before me continually; because He is at my right hand, I shall not be moved.*"

DEANNA

Literal Meaning
GODDESS; DIVINE ONE

Suggested Character Quality or Godly Characteristic
GOD'S PRINCESS
Suggested Lifetime Scripture Verse — Isaiah 60:2
"For behold, darkness shall cover the earth and a dark cloud the nations; but the Lord shall arise over you, His glory shall be seen upon you."

DEBBY

Literal Meaning
THE BEE
Suggested Character Quality or Godly Characteristic
SEEKING ONE
Suggested Lifetime Scripture Verse — Jeremiah 29:13
"You will seek Me and find Me when you will seek Me with all your heart."

Explanation:
The bee could not live unless it went out seeking for its sustenance.

DEBORAH

Literal Meaning
THE BEE
Suggested Character Quality or Godly Characteristic
SEEKING ONE
Suggested Lifetime Scripture Verse — Jeremiah 29:13
"You will seek Me and find Me when you will seek Me with all your heart."

Explanation:
See Debby

DEBRA

Literal Meaning
THE BEE
Suggested Character Quality or Godly Characteristic
SEEKING ONE
Suggested Lifetime Scripture Verse — Jeremiah 29:13
"You will seek Me and find Me when you will seek Me with all your heart."

D

Explanation:
See Debby

DELCI

Literal Meaning
DELIGHTFUL ONE-
Suggested Character Quality or Godly Characteristic
DELIGHTFUL ONE
Suggested Lifetime Scripture Verse — Psalm 37:4
"*Have your delight in the Lord and He will give you the desires of your heart.*"

DELIA

Literal Meaning
OF DELOS
Suggested Character Quality or Godly Characteristic
DELIGHTFUL ONE
Suggested Lifetime Scripture Verse — Psalm 37:4
"*Have your delight in the Lord and He will give you the desires of your heart.*"

DELORES

Literal Meaning
SORROWS
Suggested Character Quality or Godly Characteristic
COMPASSIONATE SPIRIT
Suggested Lifetime Scripture Verse — I Corinthians 13:13
"*There remain then, faith, hope, love, these three; but the greatest of these is love.*"

DENISE

Literal Meaning
ADHERENT OF DIONYSUS, GREEK GOD OF WINE
Suggested Quality or Godly Characteristic
WISE DISCERNER
Suggested Lifetime Scripture Verse — Psalm 119:140
"*Thy word is well tested; therefore Thy servant loves it.*"

Explanation:
The thought expressed here is that one must know how to discern between good and evil.

DENNIS

Literal Meaning
GOD OF WINE
Suggested Character Quality or Godly Characteristic
DISCERNER OF EXCELLENCE
Suggested Lifetime Scripture Verse — Matthew 6:33
"But you, seek first His kingdom and His righteousness and all these things will be added to you."

Explanation:
See Denise

DEREK

Literal Meaning
"RULE OF THE PEOPLE" — Germanic
Suggested Character Quality or Godly Characteristic
FULL OF JUSTICE
Suggested Lifetime Scripture Verse — Psalm 41:1
"Blessings are his, who considers the weak; in the day of misfortune the Lord will deliver him."

Explanation:
"Rule of the People" suggests one who exhibits justice.

DERYL

Suggested Character Quality or Godly Characteristic
BELOVED ONE
Suggested Lifetime Scripture Verse — Psalm 26:3
"For Thy lovingkindness is before my eyes, and I have walked in Thy truth."

DIANA

Literal Maning
DIVINE ONE

D

Suggested Character Quality or Godly Characteristic
IN GOD'S GLORY
Suggested Lifetime Scripture Verse — Isaiah 54:10
"For though the mountains should move and the hills should shake, My lovingkindness shall never depart from you nor the covenant of My peace be withdrawn, says the Lord, who has compassion upon you."

DIANE

Literal Meaning
DIVINE ONE
Suggested Character Quality or Godly Characteristic
IN GOD'S GLORY
Suggested Lifetime Scripture Verse — Isaiah 54:10
"For though the mountains should move and the hills should shake, My lovingkindness shall never depart from you, nor the covenant of My peace be withdrawn, says the Lord, who has compassion upon you."

DIANNE

Literal Meaning
GODDESS; DIVINE ONE
Suggested Character Quality or Godly Characteristic
IN GOD'S GLORY
Suggested Lifetime Scripture Verse — Isaiah 54:10
"For though the mountains should move and the hills should shake, My lovingkindness shall never depart from you nor the covenant of My peace be withdrawn, says the Lord, who has compassion upon you."

DICK

Literal Meaning
POWERFUL RULER
Suggested Character Quality or Godly Characteristic
BRAVE; STRONG
Suggested Lifetime Scripture Verse — Isaiah 12:2
"Behold, God is my salvation; I will trust and not be afraid, for Jehovah, the Lord, is my strength and my song; yes, He has become my salvation."

DOMINIQUE

Literal Meaning
BELONGING TO THE LORD
Suggested Character Quality or Godly Characteristic
BELONGING TO GOD
Suggested Lifetime Scripture Verse — Lamentations 3:25
"*The Lord is good to those who wait for Him, to the soul that seeks Him.*"

DONALD

Literal Meaning
WORLD MIGHTY, WORLD RULER
Suggested Character Quality or Godly Characteristic
OVERCOMER
Suggested Lifetime Scripture Verse — Revelation 2:7
"*Whoever has an ear, let him hear what the Spirit says to the churches. I shall grant the victor to eat from the tree of life that stands in the paradise of God.*"

DONNA

Literal Meaning
LADY
Suggested Character Quality or Godly Characteristic
DIGNITY OF CHARACTER
Suggested Lifetime Scripture Verse — Hosea 14:9
"*Whoever is wise will understand these things, and the discerning man will know them; for the ways of the Lord are right and the righteous walk in them; but transgressors stumble in them.*"

DORA

Literal Meaning
GIFT OF GOD
Suggested Character Quality or Godly Characteristic
GIFT OF GOD
Suggested Lifetime Scripture Verse — Isaiah 30:18
"*Nevertheless the Lord longs to be gracious to you! Therefore He shall rise up to bestow mercy on you; for the Lord is a God of Justice. Blessed are they who wait for Him.*"

D

DOREEN

Literal Meaning
"SULLEN" — Irish
Suggested Character Quality or Godly Characteristic
DEVOTED HEART
Suggested Lifetime Scripture Verse — Psalm 13:5
"But I have trusted in Thine unfailing love: my heart rejoices in Thy deliverance."

Explanation:
Sullen, in this case, has the connotation that one is serious about life; therefore, devotion would be characteristic of this person.

DORIS

Literal Meaning
BOUNTIFUL
Suggested Character Quality or Godly Characteristic
EXCELLENT VIRTUE
Suggested Lifetime Scripture Verse — Prov. 2:11, 12
"Discretion will protect you; discernment will guard you, to deliver you from the way of evil, from men speaking perverted things."

DOROTHY

Literal Meaning
GIFT OF GOD
Suggested Character Quality or Godly Characteristic
GIFT OF GOD
Suggested Lifetime Scripture Verse — Psalm 119:58
"Wholeheartedly I sought Thy favor; be merciful to me according to Thy word."

DOUGLAS

Literal Meaning
FROM THE BLACK OR DARK WATER
Suggested Character Quality or Godly Characteristic
SEEKER OF LIGHT
Suggested Lifetime Scripture Verse — Isaiah 60:1

"Arise, shine; for your light has come, and the glory of the Lord has risen upon you!"

Explanation:
One dwelling in a black place would seek light.

DUANE

Literal Meaning
SONG
Suggested Character Quality or Godly Characteristic
CHEERFUL OF HEART
Suggested Lifetime Scripture Verse — Habakkuk 3:18
"Yet I will rejoice in the Lord, I will joy in the God of my salvation."

DUNCAN

Literal Meaning
"BROWN WARRIOR" — Celtic
Suggested Character Quality or Godly Characteristic
LOYAL ONE
Suggested Lifetime Scripture Verse — Psalm 56:12
"On me, O God, are Thy vows; I will give Thee thank-offerings."

Explanation:
A warrior's best quality is his loyalty to his commander and country.

DUSTIN

Literal Meaning
BRAVE FIGHTER
Suggested Character Quality or Godly Characteristic
LOYAL HEART
Suggested Lifetime Scripture Verse — Psalm 34:1
"I will bless the Lord at all times; His praise shall continually be in my mouth."

DWIGHT

Literal Meaning
WHITE OR BLOND ONE

D

Suggested Character Quality or Godly Characteristic
DWELLER IN TRUTH
Suggested Lifetime Scripture Verse — Psalm 15:2, 5
"He who walks in integrity, who does what is right, and who speaks the truth in his heart; . . . He who does these things shall never be moved."

Explanation:
White corresponds with purity and honesty.

EARL

Literal Meaning
NOBLEMAN; CHIEF
Suggested Character Quality or Godly Characteristic
MAN OF HONOR
Suggested Lifetime Scripture Verse — Isaiah 30:18
"Nevertheless the Lord longs to be gracious to you! Therefore He shall rise up to bestow mercy on you; for the Lord is a God of justice. Blessed are they who wait for Him."

ED

Literal Meaning
"HAPPY" — Anglo-Saxon
Suggested Character Quality or Godly Characteristic
CHEERFUL ONE
Suggested Lifetime Scripture Verse — Psalm 43:4
"Then I will go to the altar of God, to God, the joy of my exultation, and praise Thee with the harp, O God, my God."

EDGAR

Literal Meaning
PROSPEROUS SPEARMAN
Suggested Character Quality or Godly Characteristic
COURAGEOUS HEART
Suggested Lifetime Scripture Verse — I Corinthians 15:58
"Consequently, my beloved brothers, be steadfast, immovable, at all times abounding in the Lord's service, aware that your labor in the Lord is not futile."

E

EDITH

Literal Meaning
RICH GIFT
Suggested Character Quality or Godly Characteristic
GOD'S GIFT
Suggested Lifetime Scripture Verse — Isaiah 30:18
"Nevertheless the Lord longs to be gracious to you! Therefore He shall rise up to bestow mercy on you; for the Lord is a God of Justice. Blessed are they who wait for Him."

EDMUND

Literal Meaning
CHEERFUL ONE
Suggested Character Quality or Godly Characteristic
CHEERFUL ONE
Suggested Lifetime Scripture Verse — Psalm 43:4
"Then I will go to the altar of God, to God, the joy of my exultation, and praise Thee with the harp, O God, my God."

EDNA

Literal Meaning
REJUVENATION
Suggested Character Quality or Godly Characteristic
YOUTHFUL HEART
Suggested Lifetime Scripture Verse — Psalm 71:5
"For Thou art my hope, O Lord God; Thou art my trust from my youth."

EDWARD

Literal Meaning
PROSPEROUS GUARDIAN
Suggested Character Quality or Godly Characteristic
PROSPEROUS GUARDIAN
Suggested Lifetime Scripture Verse — Psalm 37:37
"Watch the upright and observe the righteous, for there is a future to the man of peace."

EDWIN

Literal Meaning
"RICH FRIEND" — Anglo-Saxon

Suggested Character Quality or Godly Characteristic
FRIENDLY SPIRIT
Suggested Lifetime Scripture Verse — Proverbs 18:24
"*A man has many friends for companionship, but there is a friend who sticks closer than a brother.*"

EDYTH

Literal Meaning
RICH GIFT
Suggested Character Quality or Godly Characteristic
GOD'S GIFT
Suggested Lifetime Scripture Verse — Isaiah 30:18
"*Nevertheless the Lord longs to be gracious to you! Therefore He shall rise up to bestow mercy on you; for the Lord is a God of Justice. Blessed are they who wait for Him.*"

EILEEN

Literal Meaning
LIGHT
Suggested Character Quality or Godly Characteristic
LIGHT
Suggested Lifetime Scripture Verse — Psalm 37:6
"*He will bring forth your righteousness like the light, and your right as the noonday brightness.*"

ELAINE

Literal Meaning
THE LILY MAID OF ASTOLAT
Suggested Character Quality or Godly Characteristic
BRIGHT ONE
Suggested Lifetime Scripture Verse — Isaiah 62:3
"*You shall be a crown of glory in the hand of the Lord and a royal diadem in the palm of your God.*"

ELDON

Literal Meaning
Place Name—ALDER VALLEY
Suggested Character Quality or Godly Characteristic
PROSPEROUS SPIRIT

E

Suggested Lifetime Scripture Verse — Psalm 37:37
"*Watch the upright and observe the righteous, for there is future to the man of peace.*"

ELEANOR

Literal Meaning
LIGHT; BRIGHT ONE
Suggested Character Quality or Godly Characteristic
BRIGHT ONE
Suggested Lifetime Scripture Verse — Isaiah 62:3
"*You shall be a crown of glory in the hand of the Lord and a royal diadem in the palm of your God.*"

Explanation:
The light of God causes a person to radiate His presence.

ELI

Literal Meaning
HEIGHT OR ELEVATED
Suggested Character Quality or Godly Characteristic
IN GOD'S HONOR
Suggested Lifetime Scripture Verse — Psalm 5:12
"*Thou, O Lord, dost bless the righteous; as with a shield Thou dost surround him with favor.*"

ELINOR

Literal Meaning
LIGHT; BRIGHT ONE
Suggested Character Quality or Godly Characteristic
BRIGHT ONE
Suggested Lifetime Scripture Verse — Isaiah 62:3
"*You shall be a crown of glory in the hand of the Lord and a royal diadem in the palm of your God.*"

Explanation:
See Eleanor

ELISA

Literal Meaning
CONSECRATED TO GOD

Suggested Character Quality or Godly Characteristic
CONSECRATED ONE
Suggested Lifetime Scripture Verse — Psalm 119:34
"Give me understanding, and I shall observe Thy law, and keep it wholeheartedly."

ELIZABETH

Literal Meaning
CONSECRATED TO GOD
Suggested Character Quality or Godly Characteristic
CONSECRATED ONE
Suggested Lifetime Scripture Verse — Psalm 119:34
"Give me understanding, and I shall observe Thy law, and keep it wholeheartedly."

ELLA

Literal Meaning
ALL
Suggested Character Quality or Godly Characteristic
BRIGHT ONE
Suggested Lifetime Scripture Verse — Isaiah 62:3
"You shall be a crown of glory in the hand of the Lord and a royal diadem in the palm of your God."

ELLEN

Literal Meaning
BRIGHT ONE
Suggested Character Quality or Godly Characteristic
BRIGHT ONE
Suggested Lifetime Scripture Verse — Isaiah 62:3
"You shall be a crown of glory in the hand of the Lord and a royal diadem in the palm of your God."

Explanation:
See Eleanor

ELLERY

Literal Meaning
Place Name

E

Suggested Character Quality or Godly Characteristic
NOBLE SPIRIT
Suggested Lifetime Scripture Verse — Job 10:12
"Thou didst bestow upon me life and compassion; and Thy care has preserved my spirit."

ELMER

Literal Meaning
NOBLE; FAMOUS
Suggested Character Quality or Godly Characteristic
NOBLE HEART
Suggested Lifetime Scripture Verse — Psalm 112:5
"It is well with him who is generous and ready to lend, the man who conducts his business with fairness."

ELSA

Literal Meaning
CONSECRATED TO GOD
Suggested Character Quality or Godly Characteristic
CONSECRATED TO GOD
Suggested Lifetime Scripture Verse — Psalm 119:34
"Give me understanding, and I shall observe Thy law, and keep it wholeheartedly."

ELSIE

Literal Meaning
CONSECRATED TO GOD
Suggested Character Quality or Godly Characteristic
CONSECRATED TO GOD
Suggested Lifetime Scripture Verse — Psalm 119:34
"Give me understanding, and I shall observe Thy law, and keep it wholeheartedly."

ELWIN

Literal Meaning
ELFIN FRIEND
Suggested Character Quality or Godly Characteristic
FRIENDLY

Suggested Lifetime Scripture Verse — Proverbs 11:30
"The fruit of the righteous is a tree of life, and a wise man wins friends."

EMA

Literal Meaning
NURSE
Suggested Character Quality or Godly Characteristic
CARING ONE
Suggested Lifetime Scripture Verse — Jude 1:21
"Keep yourselves in the love of God, all the while awaiting the mercy of our Lord Jesus Christ for eternal life."

EMIL

Literal Meaning
INDUSTRIOUS
Suggested Character Quality or Godly Characteristic
DILIGENT ONE
Suggested Lifetime Scripture Verse — Psalm 37:3
"Trust in the Lord and do good; inhabit the land and practice faithfulness."

EMILY

Literal Meaning
INDUSTRIOUS
Suggested Character Quality or Godly Characteristic
DILIGENT ONE
Suggested Lifetime Scripture Verse — Proverbs 31:27
"She looks well to the ways of her household and eats no bread of idleness."

EMMA

Literal Meaning
NURSE
Suggested Character Quality or Godly Characteristic
CARING ONE
Suggested Lifetime Scripture Verse — Jude 1:21
"Keep yourselves in the love of God, all the while awaiting the mercy of our Lord Jesus Christ for eternal life."

E

ERIC

Literal Meaning
EVER POWERFUL; EVER RULER
Suggested Character Quality or Godly Characteristic
GODLY POWER
Suggested Lifetime Scripture Verse — Psalm 8:4, 6
"What is man that Thou art mindful of him, or the son of man that Thou carest for him? . . . Thou givest him dominion over the works of Thy hands; Thou has placed all things under his feet."

ERIKA

Literal Meaning
EVER POWERFUL
Suggested Character Quality or Godly Characteristic
WOMAN OF ESTEEM
Suggested Lifetime Scripture Verse — Habakkuk 3:19
"The Lord God is my strength; He makes my feet like hinds' feet, He makes me tread upon my high places."

ERNEST

Literal Meaning
EARNEST ONE
Suggested Character Quality or Godly Characteristic
VIGOROUS SPIRIT
Suggested Lifetime Scripture Verse — Psalm 119:40
"Truly, I yearn for Thy precepts; give me life according to Thy righteousness."

ERWIN

Literal Meaning
SEA-FRIEND
Suggested Character Quality or Godly Characteristic
FRIENDLY ONE
Suggested Lifetime Scripture Verse — Proverbs 11:30
"The fruit of the righteous is a tree of life, and a wise man wins friends."

ESTHER

Literal Meaning
A STAR
Suggested Character Quality or Godly Characteristic
HUMILITY OF SPIRIT
Suggested Lifetime Scripture Verse — Isaiah 30:15
"*For thus says the Lord God, the Holy One of Israel: In conversion and rest you shall be saved; in quietness and confidence shall be your strength.*"

Explanation:
The biblical Esther is noted for her outstanding humility of Spirit.

ETHAN

Literal Meaning
FIRM
Suggested Character Quality or Godly Characteristic
STEADFAST HEART
Suggested Lifetime Scripture Verse — I Corinthians 15:58
"*Consequently, my beloved brothers, be steadfast; immovable, at all times abounding in the Lord's service, aware that your labor in the Lord is not futile.*"

ETHEL

Literal Meaning
NOBLE ONE
Suggested Character Quality or Godly Characteristic
DIGNITY OF CHARACTER
Suggested Lifetime Scripture Verse — I Chronicles 29:17
"*But O my God, I know that Thou dost test the heart and dost take pleasure in what is right . . .*"

EUGENE

Literal Meaning
WELL-BORN; NOBLE
Suggested Character Quality or Godly Characteristic
WELL-BORN; NOBLE

E

Suggested Lifetime Scripture Verse — Psalm 91:15
"When he calls upon Me, I will answer him; I will be with him in trouble; I will rescue him and honor him."

EUGENIA

Literal Meaning
"NOBILITY" — Greek
Suggested Character Quality or Godly Characteristic
NOBLE SPIRIT
Suggested Lifetime Scripture Verse — Psalm 62:7
"My salvation and my glory depend on God; the rock of my defence, my refuge is in God."

EUNICE

Literal Meaning
HAPPY, VICTORIOUS ONE
Suggested Character Quality or Godly Characteristic
JOY WITH VICTORY
Suggested Lifetime Scripture Verse — Psalm 66:2
"Sing out to glorify His name; render Him glorious praise."

EVA

Literal Meaning
LIFE
Suggested Character Quality or Godly Characteristic
FULL OF LIFE
Suggested Lifetime Scripture Verse — Psalm 119:40
"Truly, I yearn for Thy precepts; give me life according to Thy righteousness."

EVAN

Literal Meaning
Equivalent of John
Suggested Character Quality or Godly Characteristic
GOD'S GIFT
Suggested Lifetime Scripture Verse — Isaiah 43:10
"You are my witnesses, says the Lord, and My servant whom I have chosen, in order that you may know and believe

*Me, and understand that I am He. Before Me no God was
formed, nor shall there be after Me.''*

EVE

Literal Meaning
LIFE
Suggested Character Quality or Godly Characteristic
FULL OF LIFE
Suggested Lifetime Scripture Verse — Psalm 119:40
*"Truly, I yearn for Thy precepts; give me life according
to Thy righteousness."*

EVELYN

Literal Meaning
LIGHT
Suggested Character Quality or Godly Characteristic
LIGHT
Suggested Lifetime Scripture Verse — Psalm 37:6
*"He will bring forth your righteousness like the light, and
your right as the noonday and brightness."*

EVERETT

Literal Meaning
STRONG OR BRAVE AS A BOAR
Suggested Character Quality or Godly Characteristic
MIGHTY ONE
Suggested Lifetime Scripture Verse — Proverbs 24:5
*"A wise man is strong, and a man of knowledge adds to
his strength."*

F

FAITH

Literal Meaning
BELIEF IN GOD; LOYALTY, FIDELITY
Suggested Character Quality or Godly Characteristic
TRUSTFUL
Suggested Lifetime Scripture Verse — Psalm 54:6
"With a freewill offering I will sacrifice to Thee; I will praise Thy name, O Lord, for it is good."

FAY

Literal Meaning
FAITH
Suggested Character Quality or Godly Characteristic
FULL OF TRUST
Suggested Lifetime Scripture Verse — Psalm 9:10
"Thus shall those who know Thy name trust in Thee, for Thou, O Lord, has not forsaken those who seek Thee."

FERDINAND

Literal Meaning
WORLD-DARING; LIFE-ADVENTURING
Suggested Character Quality or Godly Characteristic
LIFE-ADVENTURING
Suggested Lifetime Scripture Verse — Proverbs 19:23
"Reverence for the Lord leads to life; he who remains satisfied with that will not be visited by harm."

FERGUS

Literal Meaning
MAN-CHOICE; STRONG MAN

Suggested Character Quality or Godly Characteristic
STEADFAST SPIRIT
Suggested Lifetime Scripture Verse — I Corinthians 15:58
"Consequently, my beloved brothers, be steadfast, immovable, at all times abounding in the Lord's service, aware that your labor in the Lord is not futile."

FERN

Literal Meaning
Plant Name
Suggested Character Quality or Godly Characteristic
ABUNDANT LIFE
Suggested Lifetime Scripture Verse — Isaiah 58:11
"The Lord shall guide you continually and shall satisfy your soul in dry places; your strength shall be renewed, and you shall be like a well-watered garden, like a spring whose waters never disappoint."

FLORA

Literal Meaning
A FLOWER
Suggested Character Quality or Godly Characteristic
FRAGRANT SPIRIT
Suggested Lifetime Scripture Verse — II Corinthians 2:14
"But thanks be to God, who invariably leads us on triumphantly in Christ and evidences through us in every place the fragrance that results from knowing Him."

FLORENCE

Literal Meaning
BLOOMING, FLOURISHING, PROSPEROUS
Suggested Character Quality or Godly Characteristic
SOWER OF CHEER
Suggested Lifetime Scripture Verse — Joel 2:26
"You shall eat and be full, and be satisfied, and you shall praise the name of the Lord your God, who has done these wonders for you. My people shall never again be put to shame."

F

FLOYD

Literal Meaning
GRAY HAIRED ONE
Suggested Character Quality or Godly Characteristic
WISE ONE
Suggested Lifetime Scripture Verse — Psalm 111:10
"For reverence of the Lord is the beginning of wisdom. There is insight in all who observe it. His praise is everlasting."

FORREST

Literal Meaning
WOODSMAN
Suggested Character Quality or Godly Characteristic
STRONG; MANLY
Suggested Lifetime Scripture Verse — Joshua 1:9
"Have I not commanded you? Be resolute and strong! Be not afraid, and be not dismayed; for the Lord your God is with you everywhere you go."

FRAN

Literal Meaning
FREE ONE
Suggested Character Quality or Godly Characteristic
LIVING IN FREEDOM
Suggested Lifetime Scripture Verse — John 8:36
"So if the Son liberates you, then you are really free."

FRANCES

Literal Meaning
FREE ONE
Suggested Character Quality or Godly Characteristic
LIVING IN FREEDOM
Suggested Lifetime Scripture Verse — John 8:36
"So if the Son liberates you, then you are really free."

FRANCIS

Literal Meaning
FREE ONE
Suggested Character Quality or Godly Characteristic
LIVING IN FREEDOM

Suggested Lifetime Scripture Verse — John 8:36
"So if the Son liberates you, then you are really free."

FRANK

Literal Meaning
FREE MAN
Suggested Character Quality or Godly Characteristic
LIVING IN FREEDOM
Suggested Lifetime Scripture Verse — John 8 :36
"So if the Son liberates you, then you are really free."

FRED

Literal Meaning
PEACEFUL RULER
Suggested Character Quality or Godly Characteristic
PEACEFUL
Suggested Lifetime Scripture Verse — Philippians 4:7
"So will the peace of God, that surpasses all understanding, keep guard over your hearts and your thoughts in Christ Jesus."

FREDERIC

Literal Meaning
PEACEFUL RULER
Suggested Character Quality or Godly Characteristic
PEACEFUL
Suggested Lifetime Scripture Verse — Philippians 4:7
"So will the peace of God, that surpasses all understanding, keep guard over your hearts and your thoughts in Christ Jesus."

FREDERICK

Literal Meaning
PEACEFUL RULER
Suggested Character Quality or Godly Characteristic
PEACEFUL
Suggested Lifetime Scripture Verse — Philippians 4:7
"So will the peace of God, that surpasses all understanding, keep guard over your hearts and your thoughts in Christ Jesus."

G

GABRIEL

Literal Meaning
MAN OF GOD
Suggested Character Quality or Godly Characteristic
MAN OF GOD
Suggested Lifetime Scripture Verse — Psalm 119:73
"Thy hands have made and prepared me; give me under-standing, that I may learn Thy commandments."

GAIL

Literal Meaning
GAY, LIVELY ONE
Suggested Character Quality or Godly Characteristic
SOURCE OF JOY
Suggested Lifetime Scripture Verse — Psalm 45:7
"Thou hast loved righteousness and hated injustice, there-fore God, Thy God has anointed Thee with the oil of gladness above Thy companions."

GALEN

Literal Meaning
"CALM" — Greek
Suggested Character Quality or Godly Characteristic
CALM SPIRIT
Suggested Lifetime Scripture Verse — Psalm 31:14
"But I trust in Thee, O Lord; I said, `Thou art my God.' "

GARRET

Literal Meaning
GENTLE

Suggested Character Quality or Godly Characteristic
COURTEOUS SPIRIT
Suggested Lifetime Scripture Verse — Ephesians 4:32
*"Be kind toward one another, tenderhearted, forgiving one
another, even as God has in Christ forgiven you."*

GARY

Literal Meaning
SPEAR; SPEARMAN
Suggested Character Quality or Godly Characteristic
MAN OF LOYALTY
Suggested Lifetime Scripture Verse — II Timothy 2:4
*"No soldier gets involved in the affairs of everyday life,
so that he may please the one who enlisted him."*

GAYLE

Literal Meaning
GAY, LIVELY ONE
Suggested Character Quality or Godly Characteristic
SOURCE OF JOY
Suggested Lifetime Scripture Verse — Psalm 45:7
*"Thou hast loved righteousness and hated injustice, therefore
God, Thy God has anointed Thee with the oil of gladness
above thy companions."*

GENE

Literal Meaning
WELL-BORN; NOBLE
Suggested Character Quality or Godly Characteristic
WELL-BORN; NOBLE
Suggested Lifetime Scripture Verse — Psalm 91:15
*"When he calls upon me, I will answer him; I will be with
him in trouble; I will rescue him and honor Him."*

GENEVA

Literal Meaning
WHITE
Suggested Character Quality or Godly Characteristic
PURITY

G

Suggested Lifetime Scripture Verse — Psalm 27:4
"One thing I have asked of the Lord; that will I look for, that I may live in the house of the Lord all the days of my life, to observe the Lord's loveliness, and to meditate in His temple."

GEOFFREY

Literal Meaning
DIVINELY PEACEFUL
Suggested Character Quality or Godly Characteristic
PEACEFUL
Suggested Lifetime Scripture Verse — James 3:17
"But the wisdom from above is first of all pure, then peaceable, courteous, congenial, full of mercy and good fruits, impartial, and sincere."

GEORGE

Literal Meaning
LAND WORKER; FARMER
Suggested Character Quality or Godly Characteristic
INDUSTRIOUS
Suggested Lifetime Scripture Verse — Psalm 37:3
"Trust in the Lord and do good; inhabit the land and practice faithfulness."

GEORGENE

Literal Meaning
FARMER
Suggested Character Quality or Godly Characteristic
INDUSTRIOUS
Suggested Lifetime Scripture Verse — Proverbs 31:27
"She looks well to the ways of her household and eats no bread of idleness."

GEORGIA

Literal Meaning
FARMER
Suggested Character Quality or Godly Characteristic
INDUSTRIOUS ONE

Suggested Lifetime Scripture Verse — Proverbs 31:27
"She looks well to the ways of her household and eats no bread of idleness."

GERALD

Literal Meaning
SPEAR; MIGHTY
Suggested Character Quality or Godly Characteristic
GOD'S WARRIOR
Suggested Lifetime Scripture Verse — II Corinthians 10:4
"For the weapons of our warfare are not physical, but they are powerful with God's help for the tearing down of fortresses."

GERALDINE

Literal Meaning
SPEAR; MIGHTY
Suggested Character Quality or Godly Characteristic
APPOINTED BY GOD
Suggested Lifetime Scripture Verse — Psalm 116:13
"I will take the cup of salvation and call on the name of the Lord."

GERARD

Literal Meaning
SPEAR-BRAVE; SPEAR-STRONG
Suggested Character Quality or Godly Characteristic
LOYAL HEART
Suggested Lifetime Scripture Verse — Deuteronomy 11:1
"Love the Lord your God, therefore, and always heed His charge, His laws, His ordinances, and His commandments. Of the Lord your God's discipline you must be ever mindful."

GERTRUDE

Literal Meaning
SPEAR-STRENGTH
Suggested Character Quality or Godly Characteristic
COURAGEOUS SPIRIT

G

Suggested Lifetime Scripture Verse — Isaiah 12:2
"Behold, God is my salvation; I will trust and not be afraid, for Jehovah, the Lord, is my strength and my song; yes, He has become my salvation."

GILBERT

Literal Meaning
BRILLIANT PLEDGE OR HOSTAGE
Suggested Character Quality or Godly Characteristic
NOBLE IN HONOR
Suggested Lifetime Scripture Verse — Amos 5:24
"Let justice roll on like water, and righteousness like a mighty stream."

GILES

Literal Meaning
SHIELD-BEARER
Suggested Character Quality or Godly Characteristic
LOYAL HEART
Suggested Lifetime Scripture Verse — Deuteronomy 11:1
"Love the Lord your God, therefore, and always heed His charge, His laws, His ordinances, and His commandments. Of the Lord your God's discipline you must be ever mindful."

Explanation:
The shield bearer stayed near his master ready to obey his commands.

GINA

Literal Meaning
A QUEEN
Suggested Character Quality or Godly Characteristic
OF HUMBLE HEART
Suggested Lifetime Scripture Verse — Proverbs 15:33
"Reverence of the Lord is the instruction of wisdom, for before honor must be humility."

Explanation:
One who would truly be a queen must first be humble.

GLADYS

Literal Meaning
A PRINCESS
Suggested Character Quality or Godly Characteristic
GOD'S PRINCESS
Suggested Lifetime Scripture Verse — I Peter 2:9
"But you are a chosen race, a royal priesthood, a holy nation, a people of His acquisition, so that you may proclaim the perfections of Him who called you out of darkness into His marvelous light."

GLEN

Literal Meaning
DWELLER IN A GLEN OR VALLEY
Suggested Character Quality or Godly Characteristic
PROSPEROUS ONE
Suggested Lifetime Scripture Verse — Psalm 1:3
"He is like a tree planted by streams of water, that yields its fruits in its season, whose leaf does not wither; and everything he does shall prosper."

Explanation:
Valley suggests a place of fertility and growth.

GLENDA

Literal Meaning
VALLEY
Suggested Character Quality or Godly Characteristic
INCREASING FAITH
Suggested Lifetime Scripture Verse — Jeremiah 29:13
"You will seek Me and find Me when you will seek Me with all your heart."

Explanation:
See Glen

GLENN

Literal Meaning
DWELLER IN THE GLEN OR VALLEY
Suggested Character Quality or Godly Characteristic
PROSPEROUS ONE

G

Suggested Lifetime Scripture Verse — Psalm 1:3
"He is like a tree planted by streams of water, that yields its fruits in its season, whose leaf does not wither; and everything he does shall prosper."

Explanation:
See Glen

GLENNA

Literal Meaning
DWELLER IN A VALLEY OR GLEN
Suggested Character Quality or Godly Characteristic
INCREASING FAITH
Suggested Lifetime Scripture Verse — Jeremiah 29:13
"You will seek Me and find Me when you will seek Me with all your heart."

Explanation:
See Glen

GLORIA

Literal Meaning
GLORY; GLORIOUS ONE
Suggested Character Quality or Godly Characteristic
GLORY TO GOD
Suggested Lifetime Scripture Verse — Psalm 66:2
"Sing out to glorify His name; render Him glorious praise."

GORDON

Literal Meaning
FROM THE TRIANGULAR OR GORE-SHAPED HILL
Suggested Character Quality or Godly Characteristic
ASCENDING ONE
Suggested Lifetime Scripture Verse — Psalm 24:3-4
"Who shall go up into the mountain of the Lord; who shall stand in His holy place? He who has clean hands and a pure heart, who has not lifted up his soul to falsehood . . ."

Explanation:
Hills or mountains have always inspired men to seek ideals beyond themselves.

GRACE

Literal Meaning
THANKS
Suggested Character Quality or Godly Characteristic
THANKFUL SPIRIT
Suggested Lifetime Scripture Verse — Psalm 7:17
"*I will give thanks to the Lord according to His righteousness, and I will sing praise to the name of the Lord most high.*"

GRANT

Literal Meaning
GREAT ONE
Suggested Character Quality or Godly Characteristic
GENEROUS HEART
Suggested Lifetime Scripture Verse — Psalm 112:4
"*Light rises for the upright in times of darkness; gracious and merciful is the good man.*"

GREG

Literal Meaning
WATCHMAN; WATCHFUL ONE
Suggested Character Quality or Godly Characteristic
WATCHFUL ONE
Suggested Lifetime Scripture Verse — I Corinthians 16:13
"*Be alert; stand firm in the faith; play the man; be strong.*"

GREGORY

Literal Meaning
WATCHMAN; WATCHFUL ONE
Suggested Character Quality or Godly Characteristic
WATCHFUL ONE
Suggested Lifetime Scripture Verse — I Corinthians 16:13
"*Be alert; stand firm in the faith; play the man; be strong.*"

GUS

Literal Meaning
"STAFF" — Germanic
Suggested Character Quality or Godly Characteristic
GIVER OF SUPPORT

G

Suggested Lifetime Scripture Verse — Proverbs 6:23
"For to you the commandment is a lamp, the teaching a light, and the reproofs of discipline a way of life."

GUY

Literal Meaning
WARRIOR
Suggested Character Quality or Godly Characteristic
WATCHFUL ONE
Suggested Lifetime Scripture Verse — I Corinthians 16:13
"Be alert; stand firm in the faith; play the man; be strong."

GWEN

Literal Meaning
"WHITE" — Welsh
Suggested Character Quality or Godly Characteristic
BLESSED ONE
Suggested Lifetime Scripture Verse — Psalm 18:35
"Thou hast given me the shield of Thy salvation; Thy right hand sustains me, Thy gentleness has made me great."

Explanation:
The color white suggests receiving God's blessing.

GWENDOLYN

Literal Meaning
WHITE-BROWED ONE
Suggested Character Quality or Godly Characteristic
BLESSED ONE
Suggested Lifetime Scripture Verse — Psalm 18:35
"Thou hast given me the shield of Thy salvation; Thy right hand sustains me, Thy gentleness has made me great."

HAL

Literal Meaning
"ARMY-POWER" — Anglo-Saxon
Suggested Character Quality or Godly Characteristic
STRONG LEADER
Suggested Lifetime Scripture Verse — Joshua 1:9
"*Have I not commanded you? Be resolute and strong! Be not afraid, and be not dismayed; for the Lord your God is with you everywhere you go.*"

HANNAH

Literal Meaning
GRACE
Suggested Character Quality or Godly Characteristic
FULL OF GRACE
Suggested Lifetime Scripture Verse — Psalm 84:11
"*For the Lord God is a sun and shield; the Lord bestows mercy and honor, He holds back nothing good from those who walk uprightly.*"

HARLAN

Literal Meaning
Place Name—"ARMY-LAND"
Suggested Character Quality or Godly Characteristic
STRONG LEADER
Suggested Lifetime Scripture Verse — Joshua 1:9
"*Have I not commanded you? Be resolute and strong! Be not afraid, and be not dismayed; for the Lord your God is with you everywhere you go.*"

H

HARLEY

Literal Meaning
ARMY-MEADOW
Suggested Character Quality or Godly Characteristic
STRONG LEADER
Suggested Lifetime Scripture Verse — Joshua 1:9
"Have I not commanded you? Be resolute and strong! Be not afraid, and be not dismayed; for the Lord your God is with you everywhere you go."

HAROLD

Literal Meaning
"ARMY-RULER" — Old Norse
Suggested Character Quality or Godly Characteristic
STRONG LEADER
Suggested Lifetime Scripture Verse — Joshua 1:9
"Have I not commanded you? Be resolute and strong! Be not afraid, and be not dismayed; for the Lord your God is with you everywhere you go."

HARRIET

Literal Meaning
ARMY-POWER
Suggested Character Quality or Godly Characteristic
FULL OF WISDOM
Suggested Lifetime Scripture Verse — Proverbs 2:6
"For the Lord gives wisdom; from His mouth come knowledge and discernment."

HARRY

Literal Meaning
"ARMY-MAN" — Old English
Suggested Character Quality or Godly Characteristic
STRONG LEADER
Suggested Lifetime Scripture Verse — Joshua 1:9
"Have I not commanded you? Be resolute and strong! Be not afraid, and be not dismayed; for the Lord your God is with you everywhere you go."

HARVEY

Literal Meaning
"ARMY-WARRIOR" — Old German
Suggested Character Quality or Godly Characteristic
LOYAL
Suggested Lifetime Scripture Verse — Romans 12:9 & 10
"*Let your love be sincere, clinging to the right with abhorrence of evil. Be joined together in a brotherhood of mutual love, trying to outdo one another in showing respect.*"

HAZEL

Literal Meaning
"HAZELNUT TREE" — Old English
Suggested Character Quality or Godly Characteristic
QUIET SPIRIT
Suggested Lifetime Scripture Verse — Proverbs 15:33
"*Reverence of the Lord is the instruction of wisdom, for before honor must be humility.*"

Explanation:
The tree has always inspired men by its quiet, stately beauty.

HEATHER

Literal Meaning
"THE HEATHER FLOWER OR SHRUB"—
Middle English
Suggested Character Quality or Godly Characteristic
JOYFUL SPIRIT
Suggested Lifetime Scripture Verse — Isaiah 12:3
"*With joy, therefore, will you draw water from the fountains of salvation.*"

HEIDI

Literal Meaning
"NOBLENESS" — German
Suggested Character Quality or Godly Characteristic
FULL OF HONOR
Suggested Lifetime Scripture Verse — Hosea 14:9
"*Whoever is wise will understand these things, and the dis-*

H

cerning man will know them; for the ways of the Lord are
right and the righteous walk in them; but transgressors stumble in them."

HELEN

Literal Meaning
"LIGHT; A TORCH" — Greek
Suggested Character Quality or Godly Characteristic
BRIGHT ONE
Suggested Lifetime Scripture Verse — Psalm 37:6
"He will bring forth your righteousness like the light, and
your right as the noonday brightness."

HENRIETTA

Literal Meaning
ESTATE OR HOME RULER
Suggested Character Quality or Godly Characteristic
INDUSTRIOUS
Suggested Lifetime Scripture Verse — Proverbs 31:27
"She looks well to the ways of her household, and does not
eat the bread of idleness."

HENRY

Literal Meaning
RULER OF AN ESTATE, A HOME
Suggested Character Quality or Godly Characteristic
INDUSTRIOUS
Suggested Lifetime Scripture Verse — Colossians 3:23
"Whatever you do, work heartily as for the Lord and not
for men."

HERBERT

Literal Meaning
GLORIOUS WARRIOR
Suggested Character Quality or Godly Characteristic
DILIGENT WORKER
Suggested Lifetime Scripture Verse — Colossians 3:23
"Whatever you do, work heartily as for the Lord and not
for men."

HERMAN

Literal Meaning
"ARMY-MAN WARRIOR" — Old German
Suggested Character Quality or Godly Characteristic
MAN OF DILIGENCE
Suggested Lifetime Scripture Verse — Isaiah 12:2
"*Behold, God is my salvation; I will trust and not be afraid, for Jehovah, the Lord, is my strength and my song; He has become my salvation.*"

HILDA

Literal Meaning
"BATTLE-MAID" — Germanic
Suggested Character Quality or Godly Characteristic
WOMAN OF STRENGTH
Suggested Lifetime Scripture Verse — Psalm 17:5
"*My steps have held closely to Thy paths; my feet have not slipped.*"

HOPE

Literal Meaning
"HOPE, EXPECTATION, DESIRE" — Old English
Suggested Character Quality or Godly Characteristic
TRUSTFUL
Suggested Lifetime Scripture Verse — Job 11:18
"*You will feel confident, because you have hope; you will look around and lie down without fear.*"

HORACE

Literal Meaning
KEEPER OF THE HOURS; LIGHT OF THE SUN
Suggested Character Quality or Godly Characteristic
LOYAL AND BRAVE
Suggested Lifetime Scripture Verse — Deuteronomy 11:1
"*Love the Lord your God, therefore, and always heed His charge, His laws, His ordinances, and His commandments. Of the Lord your God's discipline you must be ever mindful.*"

H

HOWARD

Literal Meaning
"CHIEF, GUARDIAN" — Old English
Suggested Character Quality or Godly Characteristic
REASONABLE
Suggested Lifetime Scripture Verse — Isaiah 26:3
"*Thou wilt keep Him in perfect peace whose mind is stayed on Thee, because he trusts in Thee.*"

HUBERT

Literal Meaning
"BRIGHT MIND" — Germanic
Suggested Character Quality or Godly Characteristic
MAN OF HONOR
Suggested Lifetime Scripture Verse — Isaiah 30:18
"*Nevertheless the Lord longs to be gracious to you! Therefore He shall rise up to bestow mercy on you; for the Lord is a God of justice. Blessed are they who wait for Him.*"

HUGH

Literal Meaning
"MIND" — Germanic
Suggested Character Quality or Godly Characteristic
MAN OF REASON
Suggested Lifetime Scripture Verse — Psalm 32:8
"*I will instruct you and train you in the way you shall go; I will counsel you with My eye on you.*"

IAN

Literal Meaning
GOD'S GRACIOUS GIFT
Suggested Character Quality or Godly Characteristic
GOD'S GRACIOUS GIFT
Suggested Lifetime Scripture Verse — Isaiah 43:10
"You are My witnesses, says the Lord, and My servant whom I have chosen, in order that you may know and believe Me, and understand that I am He. Before Me no God was formed, nor shall there be after Me."

INGRID

Literal Meaning
"HERO'S DAUGHTER" — Old Norse
Suggested Character Quality or Godly Characteristic
INNER BEAUTY
Suggested Lifetime Scripture Verse — Psalm 11:7
"For the Lord is righteous; He loves acts of righteousness; His countenance beholds the upright."

IRENE

Literal Meaning
"PEACE" — Greek
Suggested Character Quality or Godly Characteristic
PEACEFUL SPIRIT
Suggested Lifetime Scripture Verse — John 14:27
"Peace I bequeath to you; My peace I give to you. I do not give you gifts such as the world gives. Do not allow your hearts to be disturbed or intimidated."

I

IRIS

Literal Meaning
"THE RAINBOW" — Greek
Suggested Character Quality or Godly Characteristic
GOD'S PROMISE
Suggested Lifetime Scripture Verse — Psalm 18:30
"*God! perfect is His way! The word of the Lord is proven; a shield is He to all who trust in Him.*"

Explanation:
God gave the rainbow as a sign of His promise that He would not again destroy the earth by water.

IRVING

Literal Meaning
"SEA FRIEND" — Old English
Suggested Character Quality or Godly Characteristic
FAITHFUL FRIEND
Suggested Lifetime Scripture Verse — Galatians 6:2
"*Carry one another's burden and thus fulfill the law of Christ.*"

IRWIN

Literal Meaning
SEA-FRIEND
Suggested Character Quality or Godly Characteristic
FRIENDLY ONE
Suggested Lifetime Scripture Verse — Galatians 6:2
"*Carry one another's burden and thus fulfill the law of Christ.*"

ISAAC

Literal Meaning
"LAUGHTER" — Hebrew
Suggested Character Quality or Godly Characteristic
CHEERFUL FAITH
Suggested Lifetime Scripture Verse — Psalm 16:11
"*Thou dost make me know the path of life; in Thy presence*

is fulness of joy; in Thy right hand are pleasures for evermore."

ISABEL

Literal Meaning
CONSECRATED TO GOD
Suggested Character Quality or Godly Characteristic
CONSECRATED TO GOD
Suggested Lifetime Scripture Verse — Psalm 119:34
"Give me understanding, and I shall observe Thy law, and keep it wholeheartedly."

IVA

Literal Meaning
GOD IS GRACIOUS
Suggested Character Quality or Godly Characteristic
GOD'S GRACIOUS GIFT
Suggested Lifetime Scripture Verse — Romans 6:23
"For the wages of sin is death, but the gift of God is eternal life in Christ Jesus our Lord."

IVAN

Literal Meaning
GOD IS GRACIOUS
Suggested Character Quality or Godly Characteristic
GOD'S GRACIOUS GIFT
Suggested Lifetime Scripture Verse — Romans 6:23
"For the wages of sin is death, but the gift of God is eternal life in Christ Jesus our Lord."

J

JACK

Literal Meaning
THE SUPPLANTER
Suggested Character Quality or Godly Characteristic
TRUTHFUL
Suggested Lifetime Scripture Verse — Psalm 15:2, 5
"*He who walks in integrity, who does what is right, and who speaks the truth in his heart . . . Who does not give his money for interest and who will not take a bribe against the innocent. He who does these things shall never be moved.*"

JACKIE

Literal Meaning
"THE SUPPLANTER" — Old French
Suggested Character Quality or Godly Characteristic
TRUTHFUL
Suggested Lifetime Scripture Verse — Proverbs 3:3
"*Let not lovingkindness and faithfulness leave you; bind them about your neck, write them on the tablet of your heart.*"

Explanation:
See Jacob

JACOB

Literal Meaning
"THE SUPPLANTER" — Hebrew
Suggested Character Quality or Godly Characteristic
TRUTHFUL

Suggested Lifetime Scripture Verse — Psalm 15:2, 5
"*He who walks in integrity, who does what is right, and who speaks the truth in his heart . . . Who does not give his money for interest and who will not take a bribe against the innocent. He who does these things shall never be moved.*"

Explanation:
The Lord molded Jacob of the Scriptures into a man after God's heart.

JACQUELINE

Literal Meaning
THE SUPPLANTER
Suggested Character Quality or Godly Characteristic
NOBLE IN TRUTH
Suggested Lifetime Scripture Verse — Proverbs 3:3
"*Let not lovingkindness and faithfulness leave you; bind them about your neck, write them on the tablet of your heart.*"

Explanation:
See Jacob

JAKE

Literal Meaning
"THE SUPPLANTER" — Hebrew
Suggested Character Quality or Godly Characteristic
TRUTHFUL
Suggested Lifetime Scripture Verse — Psalm 15:2, 5
"*He who walks in integrity, who does what is right, and who speaks the truth in his heart. Who does not give his money for interest and who will not take a bribe against the innocent. He who does these things shall never be moved.*"

Explanation:
See Jacob

JAMES

Literal Meaning
"THE SUPPLANTER" — Old Spanish

J

Suggested Character Quality or Godly Characteristic
TRUTHFUL
Suggested Lifetime Scripture Verse — Psalm 15:2, 5
"*He who walks in integrity, who does what is right and who speaks the truth in his heart. . . Who does not give his money for interest and who will not take a bribe against the innocent. He who does these things shall never be moved.*"

Explanation:
See Jacob

JAMIE

Literal Meaning
"THE SUPPLANTER" — Hebrew
Suggested Character Quality or Godly Characteristic
TRUTHFUL
Suggested Lifetime Scripture Verse — Proverbs 3:3
"*Let not lovingkindness and faithfulness leave you; bind them about your neck, write them on the tablet of your heart.*"

Explanation:
See Jacob

JAN

Literal Meaning
GOD IS GRACIOUS
Suggested Character Quality or Godly Characteristic
GOD'S GRACIOUS GIFT
Suggested Lifetime Scripture Verse — Isaiah 30:18
"*Nevertheless the Lord longs to be gracious to you! Therefore He shall rise up to bestow mercy on you; for the Lord is a God of justice. Blessed are they who wait for Him.*"

JANE

Literal Meaning
GOD IS GRACIOUS
Suggested Character Quality or Godly Characteristic
GOD'S GRACIOUS GIFT

Suggested Lifetime Scripture Verse — Isaiah 30:18
"Nevertheless the Lord longs to be gracious to you! Therefore He shall rise up to bestow mercy on you; for the Lord is a God of Justice. Blessed are they who wait for Him."

JANELL

Literal Meaning
GOD IS GRACIOUS
Suggested Character Quality or Godly Characteristic
GOD'S GRACIOUS GIFT
Suggested Lifetime Scripture Verse — Isaiah 30:18
"Nevertheless the Lord longs to be gracious to you! Therefore He shall rise up to bestow mercy on you; for the Lord is a God of justice. Blessed are they who wait for Him."

JANET

Literal Meaning
GOD IS GRACIOUS
Suggested Character Quality or Godly Characteristic
GOD'S GRACIOUS GIFT
Suggested Lifetime Scripture Verse — Isaiah 30:18
"Nevertheless the Lord longs to be gracious to you! Therefore He shall rise up to bestow mercy on you; for the Lord is a God of justice. Blessed are they who wait for Him."

JANICE

Literal Meaning
GOD IS GRACIOUS
Suggested Character Quality or Godly Characteristic
GOD'S GRACIOUS GIFT
Suggested Lifetime Scripture Verse — Isaiah 30:18
"Nevertheless the Lord longs to be gracious to you! Therefore He shall rise up to bestow mercy on you; for the Lord is a God of justice. Blessed are they who wait for Him."

JASON

Literal Meaning
"HEALER" — Greek

J

Suggested Character Quality or Godly Characteristic
ONE WHO HEALS
Suggested Lifetime Scripture Verse — Isaiah 61:1
"The Spirit of the Lord God is upon me; for the Lord has anointed me to preach good tidings to the humble; He has sent Me to heal the brokenhearted; to proclaim liberty to the captives and the opening of the prison to those who are bound."

JAY

Literal Meaning
"BLUE-JAY" — Old French
Suggested Character Quality or Godly Characteristic
INTEGRITY
Suggested Lifetime Scripture Verse — Proverbs 21:3
"To practice righteousness and justice is more acceptable to the Lord than sacrifice."

JEAN

Literal Meaning
GOD IS GRACIOUS
Suggested Character Quality or Godly Characteristic
GOD'S GRACIOUS GIFT
Suggested Lifetime Scripture Verse — Isaiah 30:18
"Nevertheless the Lord longs to be gracious to you! Therefore He shall rise up to bestow mercy on you; for the Lord is a God of justice. Blessed are they who wait for Him."

JEANETTE

Literal Meaning
GOD IS GRACIOUS
Suggested Character Quality or Godly Characteristic
GOD'S GRACIOUS GIFT
Suggested Lifetime Scripture Verse — Isaiah 30:18
"Nevertheless the Lord longs to be gracious to you! Therefore He shall rise up to bestow mercy on you; for the Lord is a God of justice. Blessed are they who wait for Him."

JEFFERY

Literal Meaning
"DIVINELY, PEACEFUL" — Old French

Suggested Character Quality or Godly Characteristic
PEACEFUL
Suggested Lifetime Scripture Verse — James 3:17
"But the wisdom from above is first of all pure, then peaceable, courteous, congenial, full of mercy and good fruits, without partiality, and without hypocrisy."

JENNIFER

Literal Meaning
"WHITE WAVE; WHITE PHANTOM" — Old Welsh
Suggested Character Quality or Godly Characteristic
FAIR LADY
Suggested Lifetime Scripture Verse — Proverbs 31:26
"She opens her mouth with wisdom and gentle teaching is on her tongue."

JENNY

Literal Meaning
WHITE WAVE
Suggested Character Quality or Godly Characteristic
FAIR LADY
Suggested Lifetime Scripture Verse — Proverbs 31:26
"She opens her mouth with wisdom and gentle teaching is on her tongue."

JEREMY

Literal Meaning
"APPOINTED BY JEHOVAH" — Hebrew
Suggested Character Quality or Godly Characteristic
APPOINTED BY GOD
Suggested Lifetime Scripture Verse — Isaiah 52:13
"Behold! My servant shall work wisely. He shall arise, be exalted, and shall stand exceedingly high."

JEROLD

Literal Meaning
No Literal Meaning found
Suggested Character Quality or Godly Characteristic
APPOINTED BY GOD

J

Suggested Lifetime Scripture Verse — Jeremiah 15:20
"*And I will make you to this people a fortified wall of bronze. They will fight against you, but they shall not prevail over you; for I am with you to save you and to deliver you, says the Lord.*"

JEROME

Literal Meaning
SACRED OR HOLY NAME
Suggested Character Quality or Godly Characteristic
DEVOUT HEART
Suggested Lifetime Scripture Verse — Psalm 112:1
"*Hallelujah! Oh, the bliss of the man who reveres the Lord, who greatly delights in His ordinances!*"

JERRI

Literal Meaning
SPEAR-MIGHTY
Suggested Character Quality or Godly Characteristic
CONSECRATED ONE
Suggested Lifetime Scripture Verse — Lamentations 3:24
"*The Lord is my portion, says my soul, therefore do I hope in Him.*"

JERRY

Literal Meaning
APPOINTED BY JEHOVAH
Suggested Character Quality or Godly Characteristic
APPOINTED BY GOD
Suggested Lifetime Scripture Verse — Isaiah 52:13
"*Behold! My servant shall work wisely. He shall arise, be exalted, and shall stand exceedingly high.*"

JESSE

Literal Meaning
"GOD EXISTS" — Hebrew
Suggested Character Quality or Godly Characteristic
GOD EXISTS

Suggested Lifetime Scripture Verse — Psalm 31:21
"*Blessed be the Lord, for He has shown me His lovingkindness as in an entrenched city.*"

JESSICA

Literal Meaning
WEALTHY ONE
Suggested Character Quality or Godly Characteristic
BLESSED ONE
Suggested Lifetime Scripture Verse — Psalm 119:2
"*Blessed are those who keep His testimonies, who seek Him with their whole heart.*"

JEWEL

Literal Meaning
A PRECIOUS THING OR GEM
Suggested Character Quality or Godly Characteristic
PRECIOUS ONE
Suggested Lifetime Scripture Verse — Isaiah 60:2
"*For behold, darkness shall cover the earth and a dark cloud the nations; but the Lord shall arise over you, His glory shall be seen upon you.*"

JILL

Literal Meaning
YOUTHFUL ONE
Suggested Character Quality or Godly Characteristic
YOUTHFUL HEART
Suggested Lifetime Scripture Verse — Psalm 71:17
"*O God, Thou hast taught me from my youth and I still declare Thy wonders.*"

JOAN

Literal Meaning
GOD IS GRACIOUS
Suggested Character Quality or Godly Characteristic
GOD'S GRACIOUS GIFT
Suggested Lifetime Scripture Verse — Isaiah 30:18
"*Nevertheless the Lord longs to be gracious to you! There-*"

J

fore He shall rise up to bestow mercy on you; for the Lord is a God of justice. Blessed are they who wait for Him."

JOANNA

Literal Meaning
GOD IS GRACIOUS
Suggested Character Quality or Godly Characteristic
GOD'S GRACIOUS GIFT
Suggested Lifetime Scripture Verse — Isaiah 30:18
"Nevertheless the Lord longs to be gracious to you! Therefore He shall rise up to bestow mercy on you; for the Lord is a God of justice. Blessed are they who wait for Him."

JOANNE

Literal Meaning
GOD IS GRACIOUS
Suggested Character Quality or Godly Characteristic
GOD'S GRACIOUS GIFT
Suggested Lifetime Scripture Verse — Isaiah 30:18
"Nevertheless the Lord longs to be gracious to you! Therefore He shall rise up to bestow mercy on you; for the Lord is a God of justice. Blessed are they who wait for Him."

JODI

Literal Meaning
PRAISED
Suggested Character Quality or Godly Characteristic
PRAISED OF GOD
Suggested Lifetime Scripture Verse — Lamentations 3:25
"The Lord is good to those who wait for Him, to the soul that seeks Him."

JODIE

Literal Meaning
PRAISED
Suggested Character Quality or Godly Characteristic
PRAISED OF GOD
Suggested Lifetime Scripture Verse — Lamentations 3:25

"*The Lord is good to those who wait for Him, to the soul that seeks Him.*"

JODY

Literal Meaning
PRAISED
Suggested Character Quality or Godly Characteristic
PRAISED OF GOD
Suggested Lifetime Scripture Verse — Lamentations 3:25
"*The Lord is good to those who wait for Him, to the soul that seeks Him.*"

JOE

Literal Meaning
HE SHALL ADD
Suggested Character Quality or Godly Characteristic
INCREASING FAITHFULNESS
Suggested Lifetime Scripture Verse — Proverbs 16:21
"*The wise in heart will be called a discerning man, and pleasant speech will increase learning.*"

JOEL

Literal Meaning
THE LORD IS GOD
Suggested Character Quality or Godly Characteristic
DECLARER OF GOD
Suggested Lifetime Scripture Verse — Matthew 5:16
"*Similarly let your light shine among the people so that they observe your good works and give glory to your heavenly Father.*"

JOHAN

Literal Meaning
GOD'S GRACIOUS GIFT
Suggested Character Quality or Godly Characteristic
GOD'S GRACIOUS GIFT
Suggested Lifetime Scripture Verse — Numbers 6:25
"*The Lord make His face shine upon you and be gracious to you.*"

J

JOHN

Literal Meaning
GOD IS GRACIOUS
Suggested Character Quality or Godly Characteristic
GOD'S GRACIOUS GIFT
Suggested Lifetime Scripture Verse — Numbers 6:25
"The Lord make His face shine upon you and be gracious to you."

JON

Literal Meaning
GOD IS GRACIOUS
Suggested Character Quality or Godly Characteristic
GOD'S GRACIOUS GIFT
Suggested Lifetime Scripture Verse — Numbers 6:25
"The Lord make His face shine upon you and be gracious to you."

JONAS

Literal Meaning
DOVE
Suggested Character Quality or Godly Characteristic
PEACEFUL
Suggested Lifetime Scripture Verse — Psalm 23:1-2
"The Lord is my Shepherd; I shall not lack; He makes me to lie down in green pastures."

JONATHAN

Literal Meaning
GOD IS GRACIOUS
Suggested Character Quality or Godly Characteristic
GOD'S GRACIOUS GIFT
Suggested Lifetime Scripture Verse — Numbers 6:25
"The Lord make His face shine upon you and be gracious to you."

JONETTA

Literal Meaning
No Literal Meaning Found

Suggested Character Quality or Godly Characteristic
GIFT OF GOD
Suggested Lifetime Scripture Verse — Isaiah 30:18
"Nevertheless the Lord longs to be gracious to you! Therefore He shall rise up to bestow mercy on you; for the Lord is a God of justice. Blessed are they who wait for Him."

JOSEPH

Literal Meaning
HE SHALL ADD
Suggested Character Quality or Godly Characteristic
INCREASING FAITHFULNESS
Suggested Lifetime Scripture Verse — Proverbs 16:21
"The wise in heart will be called a discerning man, and pleasant speech will increase learning."

JOSEPHINE

Literal Meaning
"HE SHALL ADD" — Hebrew
Suggested Character Quality or Godly Characteristic
INCREASING FAITHFULNESS
Suggested Lifetime Scripture Verse — Psalm 25:1-2
"To Thee; O Lord, I lift up my soul; my God, in Thee I trust, let me not be ashamed, let not my enemies triumph over me."

Explanation:
God's continual blessing suggests an increase of faith in the receiver of His attention.

JOSHUA

Literal Meaning
GOD OF SALVATION
Suggested Character Quality or Godly Characteristic
GOD IS SAVIOR
Suggested Lifetime Scripture Verse — Psalm 119:174
"I have longed for Thy salvation, O Lord; and Thy law is my delight."

J
JOY

Literal Meaning
JOYFUL ONE
Suggested Character Quality or Godly Characteristic
JOYFUL
Suggested Lifetime Scripture Verse — Psalm 16:11
"Thou dost make me know the path of life; in Thy presence is fulness of joy; in Thy right hand are pleasures for evermore."

JOYCE

Literal Meaning
JOYFUL ONE
Suggested Character Quality or Godly Characteristic
JOYFUL
Suggested Lifetime Scripture Verse — Psalm 16:11
"Thou dost make me know the path of life; in Thy presence is fulness of joy; in Thy right hand are pleasures for evermore."

JOYLYNN

Literal Meaning
JOYFUL ONE
Suggested Character Quality or Godly Characteristic
OVERFLOWING JOY
Suggested Lifetime Scripture Verse — Isaiah 55:12
"For you shall go out with joy and be led forth in peace, the mountains and the hills breaking out in song before you and all the trees of the field clapping their hands."

JUANITA

Literal Meaning
GOD'S GRACIOUS GIFT
Suggested Character Quality or Godly Characteristic
GOD'S GRACIOUS GIFT
Suggested Lifetime Scripture Verse — Isaiah 30:18
"Nevertheless the Lord longs to be gracious to you! Therefore He shall rise up to bestow mercy on you; for the Lord is a God of justice. Blessed are they who wait for Him."

JUDITH

Literal Meaning
PRAISED
Suggested Character Quality or Godly Characteristic
PRAISED OF GOD
Suggested Lifetime Scripture Verse — Lamentations 3:25
"The Lord is good to those who wait for Him, to the soul that seeks Him."

JUDY

Literal Meaning
PRAISED OF GOD
Suggested Character Quality or Godly Characteristic
PRAISED OF GOD
Suggested Lifetime Scripture Verse — Lamentations 3:25
"The Lord is good to those who wait for Him, to the soul that seeks Him."

JULE

Literal Meaning
YOUTHFUL ONE
Suggested Character Quality or Godly Characteristic
YOUTHFUL ONE
Suggested Lifetime Scripture Verse — Psalm 71:5
"For Thou art my hope, O Lord God; Thou art my trust from my youth."

JULIA

Literal Meaning
YOUTHFUL ONE
Suggested Character Quality or Godly Characteristic
YOUTHFUL ONE
Suggested Lifetime Scripture Verse — Psalm 71:5
"For Thou art my hope, O Lord God; Thou art my trust from my youth."

JULIAN

Literal Meaning
"BELONGING TO JULIUS" — Latin

J

Suggested Character Quality or Godly Characteristic
YOUTHFUL HEART
Suggested Lifetime Scripture Verse — Psalm 103:2, 5
*"Bless the Lord, O my soul, and forget not all His benefits . . .
Who satisfies you throughout life with good things so that
your youth is like the eagle's."*

JULIANA

Literal Meaning
YOUTHFUL
Suggested Character Quality or Godly Characteristic
YOUTHFUL HEART
Suggested Lifetime Scripture Verse — Psalm 71:17
*"O God, Thou hast taught me from my youth and I still
declare Thy wonders."*

JULIANNE

Literal Meaning
YOUTHFUL ONE
Suggested Character Quality or Godly Characteristic
YOUTHFUL HEART
Suggested Lifetime Scripture Verse — Psalm 71:17
*"O God, Thou hast taught me from my youth and I still
declare Thy wonders."*

JULIE

Literal Meaning
YOUTHFUL ONE
Suggested Character Quality or Godly Characteristic
YOUTHFUL ONE
Suggested Lifetime Scripture Verse — Psalm 71:5
*"For Thou art my hope, O Lord God; Thou art my trust
from my youth."*

JULIEANNE

Literal Meaning
YOUTHFUL ONE
Suggested Character Quality or Godly Characteristic
YOUTHFUL HEART

Suggested Lifetime Scripture Verse — Psalm 71:17
"O God, Thou hast taught me from my youth and I still declare Thy wonders."

JULIET

Literal Meaning
YOUTHFUL
Suggested Character Quality or Godly Characteristic
YOUTHFUL HEART
Suggested Lifetime Scripture Verse — Psalm 71:5
"For Thou art my hope, O Lord God; Thou art my trust from my youth."

JULIUS

Literal Meaning
YOUTHFUL
Suggested Character Quality or Godly Characteristic
YOUTHFUL HEART
Suggested Lifetime Scripture Verse — Psalm 103:2, 5
"Bless the Lord, O my soul, and forget not all His benefits . . . who satisfies you throughout life with good things, so that your youth is renewed like the eagles."

JUNE

Literal Meaning
BORN IN JUNE
Suggested Character Quality or Godly Characteristic
BENEVOLENT HEART
Suggested Lifetime Scripture Verse — Matthew 5:42
"Give to the one who begs from you and do not refuse the borrower."

JUSTIN

Literal Meaning
JUST
Suggested Character Quality or Godly Characteristic
FULL OF JUSTICE
Suggested Lifetime Scripture Verse — Psalm 119:66
"Teach me good taste and knowledge, for I have confidence in Thy commandments."

K

KARA

Literal Meaning
DEAR, BELOVED ONE
Suggested Character Quality or Godly Characteristic
PURITY
Suggested Lifetime Scripture Verse — Proverbs 31:30
"Charm is deceitful and beauty is passing, but a woman who reveres the Lord will be praised."

KAREN

Literal Meaning
PURE ONE
Suggested Character Quality or Godly Characteristic
PURE ONE
Suggested Lifetime Scripture Verse — Psalm 40:8
"I delight to do Thy will, my God—Thy law is deep within my heart."

KARI

Literal Meaning
PURE ONE
Suggested Character Quality or Godly Characteristic
PURE ONE
Suggested Lifetime Scripture Verse — Psalm 119:7
"I will give thanks to Thee with integrity of heart when I learn Thy righteous judgments."

KARIN

Literal Meaning
PURE ONE

Suggested Character Quality or Godly Characteristic
PURE ONE
Suggested Lifetime Scripture Verse — Psalm 40:8
"I delight to do Thy will, my God—Thy law is deep within my heart."

KARINE

Literal Meaning
PURE ONE
Suggested Character Quality or Godly Characteristic
PURE ONE
Suggested Lifetime Scripture Verse — Psalm 40:8
"I delight to do Thy will, my God—Thy law is deep within my heart."

KARL

Literal Meaning
FARMER
Suggested Character Quality or Godly Characteristic
STRONG, MANLY
Suggested Lifetime Scripture Verse — Joshua 1:9
"Have I not commanded you? Be resolute and strong! Be not afraid, and be not dismayed; for the Lord your God is with you everywhere you go."

KARLA

Literal Meaning
LITTLE WOMANLY ONE
Suggested Character Quality or Godly Characteristic
STRONG, WOMANLY
Suggested Lifetime Scripture Verse — Isaiah 41:10
"Fear not, for I am with you; be not dismayed, for I am your God! I will strengthen you, yes, I help you; yes, I will uphold you with My vindicating right hand."

KATHERINE

Literal Meaning
PURE ONE

K

Suggested Character Quality or Godly Characteristic
PURE ONE
Suggested Lifetime Scripture Verse — Psalm 119:7
"I will give thanks to Thee with integrity of heart when I learn Thy righteous judgments."

KATHI

Literal Meaning
PURE ONE
Suggested Character Quality or Godly Characteristic
PURE ONE
Suggested Lifetime Scripture Verse — Psalm 119:7
"I will give thanks to Thee with integrity of heart when I learn Thy righteous judgments."

KATHIE

Literal Meaning
PURE
Suggested Character Quality or Godly Characteristic
PURE ONE
Suggested Lifetime Scripture Verse — Psalm 119:7
"I will give thanks to Thee with integrity of heart when I learn Thy righteous judgments."

KATHRINE

Literal Meaning
PURE ONE
Suggested Character Quality or Godly Characteristic
PURITY
Suggested Lifetime Scripture Verse — Psalm 119:7
"I will give thanks to Thee with integrity of heart when I learn Thy righteous judgments."

KATHRYN

Literal Meaning
PURE ONE
Suggested Character Quality or Godly Characteristic
PURE ONE

Suggested Lifetime Scripture Verse — Psalm 119:7
"*I will give thanks to Thee with integrity of heart when
I learn Thy righteous judgments.*"

KATHLEEN

Literal Meaning
PURE
Suggested Character Quality or Godly Characteristic
PURE ONE
Suggested Lifetime Scripture Verse — Psalm 119:7
"*I will give thanks to Thee with integrity of heart when
I learn Thy righteous judgments.*"

KATHY

Literal Meaning
PURE ONE
Suggested Character Quality or Godly Characteristic
PURE ONE
Suggested Lifetime Scripture Verse — Psalm 119:7
"*I will give thanks to Thee with integrity of heart when
I learn Thy righteous judgments.*"

KATRINA

Literal Meaning
PURE
Suggested Character Quality or Godly Characteristic
PURITY
Suggested Lifetime Scripture Verse — Psalm 119:7
"*I will give thanks to Thee with integrity of heart when
I learn Thy righteous judgments.*"

KAY

Literal Meaning
PURE ONE
Suggested Character Quality or Godly Characteristic
PURE ONE
Suggested Lifetime Scripture Verse — Psalm 119:7
"*I will give thanks to Thee with integrity of heart when
I learn Thy righteous judgments.*"

K

KEITH

Literal Meaning
FROM THE BATTLE PLACE
Suggested Character Quality or Godly Characteristic
SECURE ONE
Suggested Lifetime Scripture Verse — Isaiah 12:2
"Behold, God is my salvation; I will trust and not be afraid, for Jehovah, the Lord, is my strength and my song; yes, He has become my salvation."

KELLEY

Literal Meaning
WARRIOR
Suggested Character Quality or Godly Characteristic
EXCELLENT VIRTUE
Suggested Lifetime Scripture Verse — Psalm 51:6
"Surely, Thou desirest truth in the inner self, and Thou makest me to understand hidden wisdom."

KELLY

Literal Meaning
WARRIOR
Suggested Character Quality or Godly Characteristic
EXCELLENT VIRTUE
Suggested Lifetime Scripture Verse — Psalm 51:6
"Surely, Thou desirest truth in the inner self, and Thou makest me to understand hidden wisdom."

KENDALL

Literal Meaning
FROM THE CLEAR-RIVER VALLEY OR BRIGHT VALLEY
Suggested Character Quality or Godly Characteristic
STRONG; MANLY
Suggested Lifetime Scripture Verse — Joshua 1:9
"Have I not commanded you? Be resolute and strong! Be not afraid, and be not dismayed; for the Lord your God is with you everywhere you go."

KENDRA

Literal Meaning
No Literal Meaning Found
Suggested Character Quality or Godly Characteristic
THE KNOWING WOMAN
Suggested Lifetime Scripture Verse — Proverbs 2:6
"For the Lord gives wisdom; from His mouth come knowledge and discernment."

KENNETH

Literal Meaning
HANDSOME ONE
Suggested Character Quality or Godly Characteristic
GRACIOUS; MANLY
Suggested Lifetime Scripture Verse — Psalm 37:37
"Watch the upright and observe the righteous, for there is a future to the man of peace."

KENT

Literal Meaning
WHITE, BRIGHT
Suggested Character Quality or Godly Characteristic
GRACIOUS & MANLY
Suggested Lifetime Scripture Verse — Psalm 37:37
"Watch the upright and observe the righteous, for there is a future to the man of peace."

KERMIT

Literal Meaning
FREE MAN
Suggested Character Quality or Godly Characteristic
FREE MAN
Suggested Lifetime Scripture Verse — I Corinthians 7:22
"It comes to this: the slave who is called by the Lord is the Lord's freedman; similarly he who is called while he is free is a slave of Christ."

KERRI

Literal Meaning
DARK ONE

K

Suggested Character Quality or Godly Characteristic
SEEKER OF LIGHT
Suggested Lifetime Scripture Verse — Psalm 27:8
"*In Thy behalf my heart proclaims, Seek ye My face; Thy face, Lord, I will seek.*"

Explanation:
One in darkness searches for the light.

KERRY

Literal Meaning
DARK ONE
Suggested Character Quality or Godly Characteristic
SEEKER OF LIGHT
Suggested Lifetime Scripture Verse — Psalm 27:8
"*In Thy behalf my heart proclaims, Seek ye My face; Thy face, Lord, I will seek.*"

Explanation:
See Kerri

KEVIN

Literal Meaning
GENTLE, LOVABLE
Suggested Character Quality or Godly Characteristic
KIND ONE
Suggested Lifetime Scripture Verse — Ephesians 4:32
"*Be kind toward one another, tenderhearted, forgiving one another, even as God has in Christ forgiven you.*"

KIM

Literal Meaning
CHIEF; RULER
Suggested Character Quality or Godly Characteristic
DIGNITY OF CHARACTER
Suggested Lifetime Scripture Verse — Amos 5:14
"*Seek good and not evil, that you may live; so shall the Lord, the God of Hosts, be with you, as you say.*"

KIMBALL

Literal Meaning
WARRIOR; CHIEF
Suggested Character Quality or Godly Characteristic
STRONG, ENDURING
Suggested Lifetime Scripture Verse — Proverbs 24:5
"*A wise man is strong, and a man of knowledge adds to his strength.*"

KIMBERLY

Literal Meaning
FROM THE ROYAL FORTRESS MEADOW
Suggested Character Quality or Godly Characteristic
NOBLE ONE
Suggested Lifetime Scripture Verse — Proverbs 31:25
"*Strength and dignity clothe her and she laughs at the future.*"

KIRBY

Literal Meaning
CHURCH TOWN
Suggested Character Quality or Godly Characteristic
WORSHIPFUL SPIRIT
Suggested Lifetime Scripture Verse — Jonah 2:9
"*But I will sacrifice to Thee with the voice of thanksgiving; what I have vowed, I will make good. Deliverance is the Lord's.*"

KIRK

Literal Meaning
DWELLER AT THE CHURCH
Suggested Character Quality or Godly Characteristic
WORSHIPFUL SPIRIT
Suggested Lifetime Scripture Verse — Jonah 2:9
"*But I will sacrifice to Thee with the voice of thanksgiving; what I have vowed, I will make good. Deliverance is the Lord's.*"

K

KIRSTEN

Literal Meaning
CHRISTIAN
Suggested Character Quality or Godly Characteristic
FOLLOWER OF CHRIST
Suggested Lifetime Scripture Verse — Psalm 63:8
"*My soul follows close behind Thee; Thy right hand upholds me.*"

KRIS

Literal Meaning
CHRISTIAN
Suggested Character Quality or Godly Characteristic
FOLLOWER OF CHRIST
Suggested Lifetime Scripture Verse — Psalm 63:8
"*My soul follows close behind Thee; Thy right hand upholds me.*"

KRISTA

Literal Meaning
CHRISTIAN
Suggested Character Quality or Godly Characteristic
FOLLOWER OF CHRIST
Suggested Lifetime Scripture Verse — Psalm 63:8
"*My soul follows close behind Thee; Thy right hand upholds me.*"

KRISTI

Literal Meaning
CHRISTIAN
Suggested Character Quality or Godly Characteristic
FOLLOWER OF CHRIST
Suggested Lifetime Scripture Verse — Psalm 63:8
"*My soul follows close behind Thee; Thy right hand upholds me.*"

KRISTIN

Literal Meaning
CHRISTIAN

Suggested Character Quality or Godly Characteristic
FOLLOWER OF CHRIST
Suggested Lifetime Scripture Verse — Psalm 63:8
"*My soul follows close behind Thee; Thy right hand upholds me.*"

KRISTINA

Literal Meaning
CHRISTIAN
Suggested Character Quality or Godly Characteristic
FOLLOWER OF CHRIST
Suggested Lifetime Scripture Verse — Psalm 63:8
"*My soul follows close behind Thee; Thy right hand upholds me.*"

KRISTINE

Literal Meaning
CHRISTIAN
Suggested Character Quality or Godly Characteristic
FOLLOWER OF CHRIST
Suggested Lifetime Scripture Verse — Psalm 63:8
"*My soul follows close behind Thee; Thy right hand upholds me.*"

KRISTY

Literal Meaning
CHRISTIAN
Suggested Character Quality or Godly Characteristic
FOLLOWER OF CHRIST
Suggested Lifetime Scripture Verse — Psalm 63:8
"*My soul follows close behind Thee; Thy right hand upholds me.*"

KURT

Literal Meaning
BOLD COUNSELOR
Suggested Character Quality or Godly Characteristic
ABLE TO COUNSEL
Suggested Lifetime Scripture Verse — Isaiah 1:17

K

"Learn to do good! Seek justice; restrain the ruthless; protest the orphan; defend the widow."

KYLE

Literal Meaning
FROM THE STRAIT
Suggested Character Quality or Godly Characteristic
INTEGRITY
Suggested Lifetime Scripture Verse — Psalm 91:4
"He will cover you with His feathers, and under His wings you will find protection; His faithfulness is a shield and armor."

LANA

Literal Meaning
FAIR
Suggested Character Quality or Godly Characteristic
FAIR COUNTENANCE
Suggested Lifetime Scripture Verse — Ephesians 4:32
"Be kind toward one another, tender-hearted, forgiving one another, even as God has in Christ forgiven you."

Explanation:
A person's countenance is determined by his inward attitude.

LARK

Literal Meaning
SINGING LARK OR SKYLARK
Suggested Character Quality or Godly Characteristic
A MERRY HEART
Suggested Lifetime Scripture Verse — John 15:11
"I have talked these matters over with you so that My joy may be in you and your joy be made complete."

LARRY

Literal Meaning
LAUREL-CROWNED ONE
Suggested Character Quality or Godly Characteristic
VICTOR
Suggested Lifetime Scripture Verse — I Corinthians 15:57
"But thanks be to God, who gives us the victory through out Lord Jesus Christ!"

L

LAURA

Literal Meaning
A CROWN OF LAUREL-LEAVES
Suggested Character Quality or Godly Characteristic
VICTORIOUS SPIRIT
Suggested Lifetime Scripture Verse — Lamentations 3:25
"The Lord is good to those who wait for Him, to the soul that seeks Him."

LAUREL

Literal Meaning
A CROWN OF LAUREL-LEAVES
Suggested Character Quality or Godly Characteristic
VICTORIOUS SPIRIT
Suggested Lifetime Scripture Verse — II Corinthians 2:14
"But thanks be to God, who invariably leads us on triumphantly in Christ and evidences through us in every place the fragrance that results from knowing Him."

LAURETTA

Literal Meaning
A CROWN OF LAUREL-LEAVES
Suggested Character Quality or Godly Characteristic
VICTORIOUS SPIRIT
Suggested Lifetime Scripture Verse — II Corinthians 2:14
"But thanks be to God, who invariably leads us on triumphantly in Christ and evidences through us in every place the fragrance that results from knowing Him."

LAURIE

Literal Meaning
A CROWN OF LAUREL-LEAVES
Suggested Character Quality or Godly Characteristic
VICTORIOUS SPIRIT
Suggested Lifetime Scripture Verse — I Corinthians 15:57
"But thanks be to God, who gives us the victory through our Lord Jesus Christ!"

LA VONNE

Literal Meaning
SPRING-LIKE
Suggested Character Quality or Godly Characteristic
ABUNDANT LIFE
Suggested Lifetime Scripture Verse — Psalm 52:8
"But I am like a green olive tree in the house of God; I trust in God's lovingkindness forever and ever."

Explanation:
Spring is the time of new life.

LAWREN

Literal Meaning
LAUREL-CROWNED ONE
Suggested Character Quality or Godly Characteristic
VICTORIOUS
Suggested Lifetime Scripture Verse — I Corinthians 15:57
"But thanks be to God, who gives us the victory through our Lord Jesus Christ!"

LAWRENCE

Literal Meaning
LAUREL-CROWNED ONE
Suggested Character Quality or Godly Characteristic
VICTOR
Suggested Lifetime Scripture Verse — I Corinthinas 15:57
"But thanks be to God, who gives us the victory through our Lord Jesus Christ!"

LEAH

Literal Meaning
WEARY ONE
Suggested Character Quality or Godly Characteristic
CONTENTED ONE
Suggested Lifetime Scripture Verse — Psalm 73:28
"But as for me, drawing near to God is good for me; I

L

*have made the Lord my refuge, so that I may announce
all Thy works."*

LEE

Literal Meaning
FROM THE PASTURE MEADOW
Suggested Character Quality or Godly Characteristic
PROSPEROUS ONE
Suggested Lifetime Scripture Verse — Psalm 13:6
*"Let me sing to the Lord because He has dealt generously
with me."*

LEIGH

Literal Meaning
WEARY ONE
Suggested Character Quality or Godly Characteristic
CONTENTED ONE
Suggested Lifetime Scripture Verse — Psalm 73:28
*"But as for me, drawing near to God is good for me; I
have made the Lord my refuge, so that I may announce
all Thy works."*

LENORE

Literal Meaning
BRIGHT ONE
Suggested Character Quality or Godly Characteristic
BRIGHT ONE
Suggested Lifetime Scripture Verse — Psalm 37:6
*"He will bring forth your righteousness like the light, and
your right as the noonday brightness."*

LEO

Literal Meaning
LION
Suggested Character Quality or Godly Characteristic
COURAGEOUS
Suggested Lifetime Scripture Verse — Proverbs 28:1, 12
*"The wicked flee when there is no one pursuing, but the
righteous are as fearless as a young lion. When the righteous*

rejoice, great is the glory; but when the wicked rise, men hide themselves."

LEONA

Literal Meaning
LION
Suggested Character Quality or Godly Characteristic
WOMAN OF COURAGE
Suggested Lifetime Scripture Verse — Isaiah 12:2
"Behold, God is my salvation; I will trust and not be afraid, for Jehovah, the Lord, is my strength and my song. . ."

LEONARD

Literal Meaning
LION-BRAVE
Suggested Character Quality or Godly Characteristic
FEARLESS AND STRONG
Suggested Lifetime Scripture Verse — Proverbs 28:1, 12
"The wicked flee when there is no one pursuing, but the righteous are as fearless as a young lion. When the righteous rejoice, great is the glory; but when the wicked rise, men hide themselves."

LEONE

Literal Meaning
LION
Suggested Character Quality or Godly Characteristic
WOMAN OF COURAGE
Suggested Lifetime Scripture Verse — Isaiah 12:2
"Behold, God is my salvation; I will trust, and will not be afraid; for the Lord God is my strength and my song, and He has become my salvation."

LESLEY (F)

Literal Meaning
DWELLER AT THE GRAY FORTRESS
Suggested Character Quality or Godly Characteristic
CALM SPIRIT
Suggested Lifetime Scripture Verse — Lamentations 3:26

L

"It is good if one hopes and quietly waits for the salvation of the Lord."

Explanation:
One who dwells at a fortress would feel safe and secure, therefore, calm.

LESLEY (M)

Literal Meaning
DWELLER AT THE GRAY FORTRESS
Suggested Character Quality or Godly Characteristic
CALM ONE
Suggested Lifetime Scripture Verse — Lamentations 3:26
"It is good if one hopes and quietly waits for the salvation of the Lord."

Explanation:
See Lesley (F)

LESLIE (F)

Literal Meaning
DWELLER AT THE GRAY FORTRESS
Suggested Character Quality or Godly Characteristic
CALM SPIRIT
Suggested Lifetime Scripture Verse — Lamentations 3:26
"It is good if one hopes and quietly waits for the salvation of the Lord."

Explanation:
See Lesley (F)

LESLIE (M)

Literal Meaning
DWELLER AT THE GRAY FORTRESS
Suggested Character Quality or Godly Characteristic
CALM SPIRIT
Suggested Lifetime Scripture Verse — Lamentations 3:26
"It is good if one hopes and quietly waits for the salvation of the Lord."

Explanation:
See Lesley (F)

LEWIS

Literal Meaning
"RENOWNED WARRIOR" — Germanic
Suggested Character Quality or Godly Characteristic
VICTORIOUS
Suggested Lifetime Scripture Verse — I Corinthians 15:57
"But thanks be to God, who gives us the victory through our Lord Jesus Christ!"

LILA

Literal Meaning
"DARK AS NIGHT" — Arabic
Suggested Character Quality or Godly Characteristic
PEACEFUL AND QUIET
Suggested Lifetime Scripture Verse — Matthew 5:9
"Blessed are the gentle, for they shall inherit the earth."

Explanation:
What is best about the night? The hurry and bustle of day are left behind. Quiet and peacefulness prepare one for rest.

LILLIAN

Literal Meaning
"THE LILY" — Latin
Suggested Character Quality or Godly Characteristic
PURE HEART
Suggested Lifetime Scripture Verse — Psalm 19:14
"Let the words of my mouth and the thoughts of my heart be pleasing in Thy sight, O Lord, my rock and my redeemer."

Explanation:
The lily has long been a symbol of purity.

LINDA

Literal Meaning
PRETTY ONE
Suggested Character Quality or Godly Characteristic
BEAUTY
Suggested Lifetime Scripture Verse — Psalm 29:2
"Ascribe to the Lord the glory of His name; worship the Lord in sacred adornment."

L

LIONEL

Literal Meaning
LION
Suggested Character Quality or Godly Characteristic
COURAGEOUS
Suggested Lifetime Scripture Verse — Proverbs 28:1, 12
"The wicked flee when there is no one pursuing, but the righteous are as fearless as a young lion. When the righteous rejoice, great is the glory, but when the wicked rise, men hide themselves."

LISA

Literal Meaning
CONSECRATED ONE
Suggested Character Quality or Godly Characteristic
CONSECRATED ONE
Suggested Lifetime Scripture Verse — Psalm 119:34
"Give me understanding, and I shall observe Thy law, and keep it wholeheartedly."

LIZANN

Literal Meaning
CONSECRATED ONE
Suggested Character Quality or Godly Characteristic
CONSECRATED HEART
Suggested Lifetime Scripture Verse — Psalm 119:34
"Give me understanding, and I shall observe Thy law, and keep it wholeheartedly."

LLOYD

Literal Meaning
GRAY-HAIRED ONE
Suggested Character Quality or Godly Characteristic
WISE ONE
Suggested Lifetime Scripture Verse — Psalm 111:10
"For reverence of the Lord is the beginning of wisdom. There is insight in all who observe it. His praise is everlasting."

LOIS

Literal Meaning
FAMOUS WARRIOR-MAID
Suggested Character Quality or Godly Characteristic
VICTORIOUS
Suggested Lifetime Scripture Verse — II Corinthians 2:14
"But thanks be to God, who invariably leads us on triumphantly in Christ and evidences through us in every place the fragrance that results from knowing Him."

LOLA

Literal Meaning
LITTLE WOMANLY ONE
Suggested Character Quality or Godly Characteristic
COMPASSIONATE SPIRIT
Suggested Lifetime Scripture Verse — I Corinthians 13:13
"There remain then, faith, hope, love, these three; but the greatest of these is love."

LOMA

Literal Meaning
No Literal Meaning Found
Suggested Character Quality or Godly Characteristic
TENDERHEARTED
Suggested Lifetime Scripture Verse — Matthew 5:42
"Give to the one who begs from you and do not refuse the borrower."

LORA

Literal Meaning
A CROWN OF LAUREL LEAVES
Suggested Character Quality or Godly Characteristic
VICTORIOUS SPIRIT
Suggested Lifetime Scripture Verse — Isaiah 12:2
"Behold, God is my salvation; I will trust, and will not be afraid; for the Lord God is my strength and my song, and He has become my salvation."

L

Explanation:
The crown of laurel leaves was given to the victor of the race.

LOREN

Literal Meaning
LAUREL
Suggested Character Quality or Godly Characteristic
VICTORIOUS
Suggested Lifetime Scripture Verse — I Corinthians 15:57
"But thanks be to God, who gives us the victory through our Lord Jesus Christ!"

Explanation:
The laurel was used as a symbol of victory.

LORETTA

Literal Meaning
BATTLE MAID
Suggested Character Quality or Godly Characteristic
VICTORIOUS SPIRIT
Suggested Lifetime Scripture Verse — II Corinthians 2:14
"But thanks be to God, who invariably leads us on triumphantly in Christ and evidences through us in every place the fragrance that results from knowing Him."

LORI

Literal Meaning
A CROWN OF LAUREL LEAVES
Suggested Character Quality or Godly Characteristic
VICTORIOUS SPIRIT
Suggested Lifetime Scripture Verse — Isaiah 12:2
"Behold, God is my salvation; I will trust, and will not be afraid; for the Lord God is my strength and my song, and He has become my salvation."

Explanation:
See Lora

LORNA

Literal Meaning
A CROWN OF LAUREL LEAVES

Suggested Character Quality or Godly Characteristic
VICTORIOUS SPIRIT
Suggested Lifetime Scripture Verse — Isaiah 12:2
"Behold, God is my salvation; I will trust, and will not be afraid; for the Lord God is my strength and my song, and He has become my salvation."

LORRAINE

Literal Meaning
PLACE OF LOTHAR
Suggested Character Quality or Godly Characteristic
WOMAN OF COURAGE
Suggested Lifetime Scripture Verse — Isaiah 12:2
"Behold, God is my salvation; I will trust, and will not be afraid; for the Lord God is my strength and my song, and He has become my salvation."

Explanation:
Arbitrarily chosen

LOUIS

Literal Meaning
FAMOUS WARRIOR-MAID
Suggested Character Quality or Godly Characteristic
VICTORIOUS
Suggested Lifetime Scripture Verse — I Corinthians 15:57
"But thanks be to God, who gives us the victory through our Lord Jesus Christ!"

LOUISE

Literal Meaning
FAMOUS WARRIOR-MAID
Suggested Character Quality or Godly Characteristic
VICTORIOUS
Suggested Lifetime Scripture Verse — II Corinthians 2:14
"But thanks be to God, who invariably leads us on triumphantly in Christ and evidences through us in every place the fragrance that results from knowing Him."

L

LOWELL

Literal Meaning
LITTLE BELOVED ONE
Suggested Character Quality or Godly Characteristic
BELOVED ONE
Suggested Lifetime Scripture Verse — I John 4:7
"Beloved, let us love one another, because love springs from God and whoever loves has been born of God and knows God."

LUANN

Literal Meaning
GRACEFUL BATTLE-MAID
Suggested Character Quality or Godly Characteristic
VICTORIOUS SPIRIT
Suggested Lifetime Scripture Verse — I Corinthians 15:57
"But thanks be to God, who gives us the victory through our Lord Jesus Christ!"

LUANNE

Literal Meaning
GRATEFUL BATTLE-MAID
Suggested Character Quality or Godly Characteristic
VICTORIOUS SPIRIT
Suggested Lifetime Scripture Verse — I Corinthians 15:57
"But thanks be to God, who gives us victory through our Lord Jesus Christ!"

LUCILE

Literal Meaning
LIGHT; BRINGER OF LIGHT
Suggested Character Quality or Godly Characteristic
BRINGER OF LIGHT
Suggested Lifetime Scripture Verse — Psalm 27:1
"The Lord is my light and my salvation; whom shall I fear? The Lord is the stronghold of my life; of whom shall I be afraid."

LUCILLE

Literal Meaning
LIGHT; BRINGER OF LIGHT
Suggested Character Quality or Godly Characteristic
BRINGER OF LIGHT
Suggested Lifetime Scripture Verse — Psalm 27:1
"The Lord is my light and my salvation; whom shall I fear? The Lord is the stronghold of my life; of whom shall I be afraid."

LUCY

Literal Meaning
LIGHT; BRINGER OF LIGHT
Suggested Character Quality or Godly Characteristic
BRINGER OF LIGHT
Suggested Lifetime Scripture Verse — Psalm 27:1
"The Lord is my light and my salvation; whom shall I fear? The Lord is the stronghold of my life; of whom shall I be afraid."

LUELLA

Literal Meaning
RENOWNED WARRIOR
Suggested Character Quality or Godly Characteristic
VICTORIOUS SPIRIT
Suggested Lifetime Scripture Verse — I Corinthians 15:57
"But thanks be to God, who gives us victory through our Lord Jesus Christ!"

Explanation:
A renowned warrior is a victorious one.

LUKE

Literal Meaning
LIGHT; BRINGER OF LIGHT OR KNOWLEDGE
Suggested Character Quality or Godly Characteristic
ENLIGHTENED ONE

L

" *His God correctly instructs and teaches him.* "

LUTHER

Literal Meaning
ILLUSTRIOUS WARRIOR
Suggested Character Quality or Godly Characteristic
VICTORIOUS SPIRIT
Suggested Lifetime Scripture Verse — I Corinthians 15:57
"*But thanks be to God, who gives us the victory through our Lord Jesus Christ.*"

LYDIA

Literal Meaning
"A WOMAN OF LYDIA — Latin
Suggested Character Quality or Godly Characteristic
WORSHIPER OF GOD
Suggested Lifetime Scripture Verse — Psalm 17:6
"*I have called on Thee, O God, for Thou wilt answer me. Incline Thine ear to me; hear my words.*"

Explanation:
The Lydia of the Bible was noted as a worshiper of God.

LYNDA

Literal Meaning
PRETTY ONE
Suggested Character Quality or Godly Characteristic
INNER BEAUTY
Suggested Lifetime Scripture Verse — Psalm 29:2
"*Ascribe to the Lord the glory of His name, worship the Lord in sacred adornment.*"

LYNETTE

Literal Meaning
FROM THE POOL OR WATERFALL
Suggested Character Quality or Godly Characteristic
REFRESHING ONE
Suggested Lifetime Scripture Verse — John 7:38

"*He who believes in Me, just as the scripture says, streams of water will flow from his innermost being.*"

LYNN

Literal Meaning
FROM THE POOL OR WATERFALL
Suggested Character Quality or Godly Characteristic
REFRESHING ONE
Suggested Lifetime Scripture Verse — John 7:38
"*He who believes in Me, just as the scripture says, streams of water will flow from his innermost being.*"

LYNNE

Literal Meaning
FROM THE POOL OR WATERFALL
Suggested Character Quality or Godly Characteristic
REFRESHING ONE
Suggested Lifetime Scripture Verse — John 7:38
"*He who believes in Me, just as the scripture says, streams of water will flow from his innermost being.*"

M

MABEL

Literal Meaning
LOVABLE
Suggested Character Quality or Godly Characteristic
LOVING HEART
Suggested Lifetime Scripture Verse — Psalm 42:1
"*As a deer pants for water brooks so my soul longs for Thee, O God.*"

MADELINE

Literal Meaning
WOMAN OF MAGDALA
Suggested Character Quality or Godly Characteristic
TRANSFORMED HEART
Suggested Lifetime Scripture Verse — Colossians 3:10
"*. . . Put on the new self who is being renewed in a full knowledge in the likeness of Him who created him.*"

Explanation:
The woman of Magdala, Mary, was remembered for the transformation that Jesus worked in her life.

MALCOLM

Literal Meaning
DISCIPLE OF COLUMBIA
Suggested Character Quality or Godly Characteristic
TEACHABLE SPIRIT
Suggested Lifetime Scripture Verse — Psalm 16:7
"*I will bless the Lord who has counseled me; even in the night my emotions admonish me.*"

Explanation:
A disciple is one who wishes to learn.

MANUEL

Literal Meaning
GOD WITH US
Suggested Character Quality or Godly Characteristic
GOD WITH US
Suggested Lifetime Scripture Verse — Psalm 5:12
"For Thou, O Lord, dost bless the righteous; as with a shield Thou dost surround him with favor."

MARA

Literal Meaning
MYRRH
Suggested Character Quality or Godly Characteristic
LIVING FRAGRANCE
Suggested Lifetime Scripture Verse — Psalm 116:17
"I will offer to Thee the sacrifice of thanksgiving and call on the name of the Lord."

Explanation:
See Miriam

MARC

Literal Meaning
GOD OF WAR
Suggested Character Quality or Godly Characteristic
MIGHTY WARRIOR
Suggested Lifetime Scripture Verse — Psalm 29:1
"Give to the Lord, O you sons of the mighty, give to the Lord glory and strength."

MARCIA

Literal Meaning
GOD OF WAR
Suggested Character Quality or Godly Characteristic
A BRAVE HEART
Suggested Lifetime Scripture Verse — Psalm 9:1

M

"I will praise the Lord with my whole heart; I will tell of all Thy marvelous works."

MARCY

Literal Meaning
GOD OF WAR
Suggested Character Quality or Godly Characteristic
A BRAVE HEART
Suggested Lifetime Scripture Verse — Psalm 9:1
"I will praise the Lord with my whole heart; I will tell of all Thy marvelous works."

MARGARET

Literal Meaning
A PEARL
Suggested Character Quality or Godly Characteristic
A PEARL
Suggested Lifetime Scripture Verse — Matthew 5:8
"Blessed are the pure in heart, for they shall see God."

MARIA

Literal Meaning
MYRRH
Suggested Character Quality or Godly Characteristic
LIVING FRAGRANCE
Suggested Lifetime Scripture Verse — Psalm 116:17
"I will offer to Thee the sacrifice of thanksgiving and call on the name of the Lord."

Explanation:
See Miriam

MARIAN

Literal Meaning
MYRRH
Suggested Character Quality or Godly Characteristic
LIVING FRAGRANCE
Suggested Lifetime Scripture Verse — Psalm 116:17

"I will offer to Thee the sacrifice of thanksgiving and call on the name of the Lord."

Explanation:
See Miriam

MARIBETH

Literal Meaning
MYRRH
Suggested Character Quality or Godly Characteristic
LIVING FRAGRANCE
Suggested Lifetime Scripture Verse — Psalm 116:17
"I will offer to Thee the sacrifice of thanksgiving and call on the name of the Lord."

Explanation:
See Miriam

MARIE

Literal Meaning
MYRRH
Suggested Character Quality or Godly Characteristic
LIVING FRAGRANCE
Suggested Lifetime Scripture Verse — Psalm 116:17
"I will offer to Thee the sacrifice of thanksgiving and call on the name of the Lord."
Explanation:
See Miriam

MARIETTA

Literal Meaning
MYRRH
Suggested Character Quality or Godly Characteristic
LIVING FRAGRANCE
Suggested Lifetime Scripture Verse — Psalm 116:17
"I will offer to Thee the sacrifice of thanksgiving and call on the name of the Lord."
Explanation:
See Miriam

M

MARILEE

Literal Meaning
MYRRH
Suggested Character Quality or Godly Characteristic
LIVING FRAGRANCE
Suggested Lifetime Scripture Verse — Psalm 116:17
"I will offer to Thee the sacrifice of thanksgiving and call on the name of the Lord."

Explanation:
See Miriam

MARILOU

Literal Meaning
MYRRH
Suggested Character Quality or Godly Characteristic
LIVING FRAGRANCE
Suggested Lifetime Scripture Verse — Psalm 116:17
"I will offer to Thee the sacrifice of thanksgiving and call on the name of the Lord."

Explanation:
See Miriam

MARILYN

Literal Meaning
MYRRH
Suggested Character Quality or Godly Characteristic
LIVING FRAGRANCE
Suggested Lifetime Scripture Verse — Psalm 116:17
"I will offer to Thee the sacrifice of thanksgiving and call on the name of the Lord."

Explanation:
See Miriam

MARK

Literal Meaning
WARLIKE ONE
Suggested Character Quality or Godly Characteristic
MIGHTY WARRIOR

Suggested Lifetime Scripture Verse — Psalm 29:1
"*Give to the Lord, O you sons of the mighty, give to the Lord glory and strength.*"

MARLENE

Literal Meaning
MYRRH
Suggested Character Quality or Godly Characteristic
LIVING FRAGRANCE
Suggested Lifetime Scripture Verse — Psalm 116:17
"*I will offer to Thee the sacrifice of thanksgiving and call on the name of the Lord.*"

Explanation:
See Miriam

MARSHALL

Literal Meaning
STEWARD
Suggested Character Quality or Godly Characteristic
LOYAL ONE
Suggested Lifetime Scripture Verse — Proverbs 3:5-6
"*Trust in the Lord with all your heart and lean not on your own understanding; in all your ways acknowledge Him, and He will direct your paths.*"

MARTHA

Literal Meaning
A LADY
Suggested character Quality or Godly Characteristic
WOMAN OF DISCRETION
Suggested Lifetime Scripture Verse — Proverbs 15:33
"*Reverence of the Lord is the instruction of wisdom, for before honor must be humility.*"

MARTIN

Literal Meaning
WARLIKE ONE
Suggested Character Quality or Godly Characteristic
LOYAL SPIRIT

M

Suggested Lifetime Scripture Verse — Psalm 112:7
"He need never fear any evil report; his heart will remain firm, fully trusting in the Lord."

MARY

Literal Meaning
MYRRH
Suggested Character Quality or Godly Characteristic
LIVING FRAGRANCE
Suggested Lifetime Scripture Verse — Psalm 116:17
"I will offer to Thee the sacrifice of thanksgiving and call on the name of the Lord."

Explanation:
See Miriam

MARVEL

Literal Meaning
WONDERFUL
Suggested Character Quality or Godly Characteristic
A MIRACLE
Suggested Lifetime Scripture Verse — Psalm 9:1
"I will praise the Lord with my whole heart; I will tell of all Thy marvelous works."

MARVIN

Literal Meaning
"FAMOUS FRIEND" — Anglo-Saxon
Suggested Character Quality or Godly Characteristic
FRIENDLY SPIRIT
Suggested Lifetime Scripture Verse — Proverbs 18:24
"A man has many friends for companionship, but there is a friend who sticks closer than a brother."

MATT

Literal Meaning
GIFT OF THE LORD
Suggested Character Quality or Godly Characteristic
GIFT OF THE LORD
Suggested Lifetime Scripture Verse — Numbers 6:25

"The Lord make His face shine upon you and be gracious to you."

MATTHEW

Literal Meaning
GIFT OF JEHOVAH
Suggested Character Quality or Godly Characteristic
GIFT OF THE LORD
Suggested Lifetime Scripture Verse — Numbers 6:25
"The Lord make His face shine upon you and be gracious to you."

MAY

Literal Meaning
GREAT ONE
Suggested Character Quality or Godly Characteristic
ESTEEMED ONE
Suggested Lifetime Scripture Verse — Proverbs 31:31
"Acknowledge the product of her hands; let her works praise her in the gates."

MAYNARD

Literal Meaning
INTENSE STRENGTH
Suggested Character Quality or Godly Characteristic
STEADFAST SPIRIT
Suggested Lifetime Scripture Verse — I Corinthians 15:58
"Consequently, my beloved brothers, be steadfast, immovable, at all times abounding in the Lord's service, aware that your labor in the Lord is not futile."

MAX

Literal Meaning
GREATEST
Suggested Character Quality or Godly Characteristic
FULL OF HONOR
Suggested Lifetime Scripture Verse — Psalm 112:6, 7
"Such a man will never be laid low, for the just shall be held in remembrance forever. He need never fear any evil

M

report; his heart will remain firm, fully trusting in the Lord."

MAXWELL

Literal Meaning
GREAT
Suggested Character Quality or Godly Characteristic
FULL OF HONOR
Suggested Lifetime Scripture Verse — Psalm 112:6, 7
"Such a man will never be laid low, for the just shall be held in remembrance forever. He need never fear any evil report; his heart will remain firm, fully trusting in the Lord."

MEG

Literal Meaning
A PEARL
Suggested Character Quality or Godly Characteristic
A PEARL
Suggested Lifetime Scripture Verse — Matthew 5:8
"Blessed are the pure in heart, for they shall see God."

MELANIE

Literal Meaning
DARK
Suggested Character Quality or Godly Characteristic
RESOLUTE COURAGE
Suggested Lifetime Scripture Verse — Nahum 1:7
"The Lord is good, a stronghold in the day of trouble; He knows those who commit themselves to Him."

Explanation:
Arbitrarily chosen

MELINDA

Literal Meaning
BEAUTIFUL, PRETTY
Suggested Character Quality or Godly Characteristic
GRACIOUS SPIRIT
Suggested Lifetime Scripture Verse — Hebrews 12:28
"Let us, therefore, be grateful that the kingdom we have

received cannot be shaken, and so let us serve God acceptably with reverence and awe."

MELODY

Literal Meaning
SONG
Suggested Character Quality or Godly Characteristic
JOYFUL LIFE
Suggested Lifetime Scripture Verse — Isaiah 12:3
"With joy, therefore, will you draw water from the fountains of salvation."

MELVIN

Literal Meaning
CHIEF
Suggested Character Quality or Godly Characteristic
RELIABLE
Suggested Lifetime Scripture Verse — Micah 6:8
"He has declared to you, O man, what is good, and what does the Lord require of you but to do justice, and to love mercy and to walk humbly with your God?"

MEREDITH

Literal Meaning
GUARDIAN FROM THE SEA
Suggested Character Quality or Godly Characteristic
BLESSED OF GOD
Suggested Lifetime Scripture Verse — Isaiah 48:17
"Thus says the Lord, your Redeemer, the Holy One of Israel: I am the Lord your God, who teaches you for your profit, who leads you in the way you should go."

MERLIN

Literal Meaning
SEA
Suggested Character Quality or Godly Characteristic
GENEROUS SPIRIT
Suggested Lifetime Scripture Verse — Psalm 40:10
"Thy righteousness I have not hid away in my heart; Thy

faithfulness and Thy salvation I have proclaimed; I have not concealed Thy lovingkindness and Thy truth from the great assembly."

Explanation:
The sea suggests deepness and openness, "generosity."

MERRI

Literal Meaning
HAPPY, JOYFUL
Suggested Character Quality or Godly Characteristic
CHEERFUL HEART
Suggested Lifetime Scripture Verse — Isaiah 12:3
"*With joy, therefore, will you draw water from the fountains of salvation.*"

MIA

Literal Meaning
MINE
Suggested Character Quality or Godly Characteristic
BELONGING TO GOD
Suggested Lifetime Scripture Verse — Lamentations 3:25
"*The Lord is good to those who wait for Him, to the soul that seeks Him.*"

Explanation:
God calls us His own.

MICHAEL

Literal Meaning
WHO IS LIKE GOD
Suggested Character Quality or Godly Characteristic
GODLINESS
Suggested Lifetime Scripture Verse — I Timothy 4:8
"*. . . Godliness is beneficial in every way; it holds promise for this present and for the future life.*"

MICHELE

Literal Meaning
WHO IS LIKE GOD

Suggested Character Quality or Godly Characteristic
GODLINESS
Suggested Lifetime Scripture Verse — Isaiah 26:7
*"For the just the way is level. Thou, Upright One, makest
smooth the path of the righteous."*

MICHELLE

Literal Meaning
WHO IS LIKE GOD
Suggested Character Quality or Godly Characteristic
GODLY WOMAN
Suggested Lifetime Scripture Verse — Isaiah 26:7
*"For the just the way is level. Thou, Upright One, makest
smooth the path of the righteous."*

MIKE

Literal Meaning
GODLIKE
Suggested Character Quality or Godly Characteristic
GODLINESS
Suggested Lifetime Scripture Verse — I Timothy 4:8
*"Because while physical training is of a little benefit, godli-
ness is beneficial in every way; it holds promise for this
present and for the future life."*

MILDRED

Literal Meaning
MILD COUNSELOR
Suggested Character Quality or Godly Characteristic
GENTLE ONE
Suggested Lifetime Scripture Verse — Colossians 3:12
*"Therefore, as God's chosen, set apart and enjoying His
love, clothe yourselves with tenderness of heart, kindliness,
humility, gentlemen, patient endurance."*

MILTON

Literal Meaning
DWELLER AT THE MILL-TOWN

M

Suggested Character Quality or Godly Characteristic
PROSPEROUS ONE
Suggested Lifetime Scripture Verse — Psalm 13:6
"*Let me sing to the Lord because He has dealt generously
with me.*"

MIRIAM

Literal Meaning
MYRRH
Suggested Character Quality or Godly Characteristic
LIVING FRAGRANCE
Suggested Lifetime Scripture Verse — Psalm 116:17
"*I will offer to Thee the sacrifice of thanksgiving and call
on the name of the Lord.*"

Explanation:
Myrrh was an incense used in the worship of God.

MITCHELL

Literal Meaning
WHO IS LIKE GOD
Suggested Character Quality or Godly Characteristic
GODLINESS
Suggested Lifetime Scripture Verse — I Timothy 4:8
"*. . . Godliness is beneficial in every way; it holds promise
for this present and for the future life.*"

MOLLY

Literal Meaning
MYRRH
Suggested Character Quality or Godly Characteristic
LIVING FRAGRANCE
Suggested Lifetime Scripture Verse — Psalm 116:17
"*I will offer to Thee the sacrifice of thanksgiving and call
on the name of the Lord.*"

Explanation:
See Miriam

MONICA
Literal Meaning
ADVISE

Suggested Character Quality or Godly Characteristic
WOMAN OF WISDOM
Suggested Lifetime Scripture Verse — Proverbs 2:6
"For the Lord gives wisdom; from His mouth come knowledge and discernment."

MORRIS

Literal Meaning
DARK-COMPLEXIONED ONE
Suggested Character Quality or Godly Characteristic
SINCERE DEVOTION
Suggested Lifetime Scripture Verse — Psalm 112:1
"Praise ye the Lord. Blessed is the man that feareth the Lord, that delighteth greatly in His commandments."

Explanation:
Arbitrarily chosen.

MOSES

Literal Meaning
SAVED
Suggested Character Quality or Godly Characteristic
DELIVERED BY GOD
Suggested Lifetime Scripture Verse — Psalm 50:23
" He who offers a sacrifice of praise honors Me: to him who prepares his way I will show the salvation of God."

MURIEL

Literal Meaning
SEA-BRIGHT
Suggested Character Quality or Godly Characteristic
BRIGHT WITH JOY
Suggested Lifetime Scripture Verse — Isaiah 12:3
"With joy, therefore, will you draw water from the fountains of salvation."

MURRAY

Literal Meaning
"MERRY" — English

M

Suggested Character Quality or Godly Characteristic
CHEERFUL SPIRIT
Suggested Lifetime Scripture Verse — Psalm 18:49
"Therefore I will extol Thee among the nations, O Lord, and will sing praises to Thy name."

MYRNA

Literal Meaning
"POLITE, GENTLE" — Gaelic
Suggested Character Quality or Godly Characteristic
GENTLE SPIRIT
Suggested Lifetime Scripture Verse — Psalm 52:8
"But I am like a green olive tree in the house of God; I trust in God's lovingkindness for ever and ever."

MYRTLE

Literal Meaning
THE MYRTLE
Suggested Character Quality or Godly Characteristic
FULL OF PRAISE
Suggested Lifetime Scripture Verse — Isaiah 55:12
"For you shall go out with joy and be led forth in peace, the mountains and the hills breaking out in song before you and all the trees of the field clapping their hands."

Explanation:
The Myrtle tree was often used to signify thanksgiving in biblical times.

NADINE

Literal Meaning
HOPE
Suggested Character Quality or Godly Characteristic
HOPEFUL ONE
Suggested Lifetime Scripture Verse — Isaiah 26:4
"*Trust in the Lord forever, for the Lord God is the Rock of Ages.*"

NAN

Literal Meaning
GRACE
Suggested Character Quality or Godly Characteristic
GRACIOUS ONE
Suggested Lifetime Scripture Verse — Hebrews 12:28
"*Let us have grace, whereby we may serve God acceptably with reverence and godly fear.*"

NANCY

Literal Meaning
GRACE
Suggested Character Quality or Godly Characteristic
GRACIOUS ONE
Suggested Lifetime Scripture Verse — Hebrews 12:28
"*Let us have grace, whereby we may serve God acceptably with reverence and godly fear.*"

NAOMI

Literal Meaning
THE PLEASANT ONE

N

Suggested Character Quality or Godly Characteristic
PLEASANT SPIRIT
Suggested Lifetime Scripture Verse — Proverbs 16:24
"*Pleasant words are as a honeycomb, sweet to the soul and
healing to the bones.*"

NATALIE

Literal Meaning
"BIRTHDAY OF CHRIST" — Latin
Suggested Character Quality or Godly Characteristic
JOYOUS SPIRIT
Suggested Lifetime Scripture Verse — Psalm 9:2
"*I will be glad and rejoice in Thee, I will sing praise to Thy
name, O most High.*"

Explanation:
The season of Christ's birthday is characterized by joy.

NATHAN

Literal Meaning
A GIFT
Suggested Character Quality or Godly Characteristic
GIVEN OF GOD
Suggested Lifetime Scripture Verse — Isaiah 43:10
"*You are My witnesses, says the Lord, and My servant whom
I have chosen, in order that you may know and believe
Me, and understand that I am He. Before Me no God was
formed, nor shall there be after Me.*"

NATHANIEL

Literal Meaning
A GIFT
Suggested Character Quality or Godly Characteristic
GIVEN OF GOD
Suggested Lifetime Scripture Verse — Isaiah 43:10
"*You are My witnesses, says the Lord, and My servant whom
I have chosen, in order that you may know and believe
Me, and understand that I am He. Before Me no god was
formed, nor shall there be after Me.*"

NEAL

Literal Meaning
CHAMPION
Suggested Character Quality or Godly Characteristic
CHAMPION
Suggested Lifetime Scripture Verse — Philippians 3:14
"*I push on to the goal for the prize of God's heavenly call in Christ Jesus.*"

NEIL

Literal Meaning
CHAMPION
Suggested Character Quality or Godly Characteristic
CHAMPION
Suggested Lifetime Scripture Verse — Philippians 3:14
"*I push on to the goal for the prize of God's heavenly call in Christ Jesus.*"

NELSON

Literal Meaning
SON OF NEIL
Suggested Character Quality or Godly Characteristic
CHAMPION
Suggested Lifetime Scripture Verse — Philippians 3:14
"*I push on to the goal for the prize of God's heavenly call in Christ Jesus.*"

NICHOLAS

Literal Meaning
"VICTORY OF THE PEOPLE" — Greek
Suggested Character Quality or Godly Characteristic
VICTORIOUS SPIRIT
Suggested Lifetime Scripture Verse — Psalm 18:46
"*The Lord lives; blessed be my rock, and exalted be the God of my salvation.*"

NICK

Literal Meaning

N

"VICTORY OF THE PEOPLE"—Greek
Suggested Character Quality or Godly Characteristic
VICTORIOUS SPIRIT
Suggested Lifetime Scripture Verse — Psalm 18:46
"The Lord lives; blessed be my rock, and exalted be the God of my salvation."

NICOLE

Literal Meaning
VICTORY OF THE PEOPLE
Suggested Character Quality or Godly Characteristic
VICTORIOUS HEART
Suggested Lifetime Scripture Verse — Job 23:11
"My feet have stayed steady in His path; I have kept His way and have never swerved aside."

NOBLE

Literal Meaning
WELL-KNOWN AND NOBLE
Suggested Character Quality or Godly Characteristic
MAN OF HONOR
Suggested Lifetime Scripture Verse — Psalm 112:6
"Such a man will never be laid low, for the just shall be held in remembrance for ever."

NOEL

Literal Meaning
"BIRTHDAY OF CHRIST" — French
Suggested Character Quality or Godly Characteristic
JOYFUL SPIRIT
Suggested Lifetime Scripture Verse — Psalm 9:1
"I will praise the Lord with my whole heart; I will tell of all Thy marvelous works."

NORA

Literal Meaning
NOBLE
Suggested Character Quality or Godly Characteristic

FULL OF HONOR
Suggested Lifetime Scripture Verse — Lamentations 3:26
*"It is good if one hopes and quietly waits for the salvation
of the Lord."*

NORBERT

Literal Meaning
BRILLIANT ONE
Suggested Character Quality or Godly Characteristic
IN GOD'S LIGHT
Suggested Lifetime Scripture Verse — Psalm 16:8
*"I have placed the Lord before me continually; because
He is at my right hand, I shall not be moved."*

NORMA

Literal Meaning
A RULE; A PATTERN OR PRECEPT
Suggested Character Quality or Godly Characteristic
EXAMPLES OF GODLINESS
Suggested Lifetime Scripture Verse — I Timothy 4:8
*". . . Godliness is beneficial in every way; it holds promise
for this present and for the future life."*

NORMAN

Literal Meaning
A NORTHMAN
Suggested Character Quality or Godly Characteristic
STRONG; MANLY
Suggested Lifetime Scripture Verse — Joshua 1:9
*"Have I not commanded you? Be resolute and strong! Be
not afraid, and be not dismayed; for the Lord your God
is with you everywhere you go."*

NORRIS

Literal Meaning
NURSE" — Occupational Name
Suggested Character Quality or Godly Characteristic
HELPFUL SPIRIT
Suggested Lifetime Scripture Verse — Romans 15:14

N

"I myself am convinced about you, my brothers, that you are full of goodness, amply furnished with knowledge, and competent to advise one another."

OLIVE

Literal Meaning
OLIVE TREE OR OLIVE BRANCH
Suggested Character Quality or Godly Characteristic
PEACEFUL SPIRIT
Suggested Lifetime Scripture Verse — Proverbs 16:24
"Pleasant words are as an honeycomb, sweet to the soul, and health to the bones."

OLIVER

Literal Meaning
"OLIVE TREE" — Latin
Suggested Character Quality or Godly Characteristic
PEACEFUL HEART
Suggested Lifetime Scripture Verse — Philippians 4:7
"So will the peace of God, that surpasses all understanding, keep guard over your hearts and your thoughts in Christ Jesus."

OLIVIA

Literal Meaning
OLIVE BRANCH
Suggested Character Quality or Godly Characteristic
PEACEFUL SPIRIT
Suggested Lifetime Scripture Verse — Proverbs 16:24
"Pleasant words are as a honeycomb, sweet to the soul and healing to the bones."

ORA

Literal Meaning
GOLDEN

O

Suggested Character Quality or Godly Characteristic
GOOD HEART
Suggested Lifetime Scripture Verse — Ephesians 4:32
"Be kind toward one another, tenderhearted, forgiving one another, even as God has in Christ forgiven you."

Explanation:
A heart of gold is a good heart.

ORIN

Literal Meaning
PINE
Suggested Character Quality or Godly Characteristic
STEADFAST ENDURANCE
Suggested Lifetime Scripture Verse — I Corinthians 15:58
"Be steadfast, immovable, at all times abounding in the Lord's service, aware that your labor in the Lord is not futile."

OSCAR

Literal Meaning
DIVINE SPIRIT
Suggested Character Quality or Godly Characteristic
BLESSED IN SERVICE
Suggested Lifetime Scripture Verse — Psalm 5:12
"Thou, O Lord, dost bless the righteous; as with a shield thou dost surround him with favor."

OWEN

Literal Meaning
"YOUTH" — Welsh
Suggested Character Quality or Godly Characteristic
YOUTHFUL HEART
Suggested Lifetime Scripture Verse — Psalm 103:2, 5
"Bless the Lord, O my soul, and forget not all His benefits, . . . who satisfies you throughout life with good things, so that your youth is renewed like the eagle's."

PAIGE

Literal Meaning
ATTENDANT
Suggested Character Quality or Godly Characteristic
OBEDIENT SPIRIT
Suggested Lifetime Scripture Verse — Proverbs 15:33
"Reverence of the Lord is the instruction of wisdom, for before honor must be humility."

PAMELA

Literal Meaning
ALL HONEY
Suggested Character Quality or Godly Characteristic
SWEET SPIRIT
Suggested Lifetime Scripture Verse — Proverbs 16:24
"Pleasant words are as a honeycomb, sweet to the soul and healing to the bones."

PAT (F)

Literal Meaning
NOBLE ONE
Suggested Character Quality or Godly Characteristic
FULL OF HONOR
Suggested Lifetime Scripture Verse — Psalm 62:7
"My salvation and my glory depend on God; the rock of my defence, my refuge is in God."

PAT (M)

Literal Meaning
"OF NOBLE BIRTH" — Latin

P

Suggested Character Quality or Godly Characteristic
FULL OF HONOR
Suggested Lifetime Scripture Verse — Psalm 26:3
"For Thy lovingkindness is before my eyes, and I have walked in Thy truth."

PATRICIA

Literal Meaning
NOBLE ONE
Suggested Character Quality or Godly Characteristic
FULL OF HONOR
Suggested Lifetime Scripture Verse — Psalm 62:7
"My salvation and my glory depend on God; the rock of my defence, my refuge is in God."

PATRICK

Literal Meaning
NOBLE ONE
Suggested Character Quality or Godly Characteristic
FULL OF HONOR
Suggested Lifetime Scripture Verse — Psalm 62:7
"My salvation and my glory depend on God; the rock of my defence, my refuge is in God."

PAUL

Literal Meaning
LITTLE
Suggested Character Quality or Godly Characteristic
DEPENDENT ON GOD
Suggested Lifetime Scripture Verse — Psalm 73:28
"But as for me, drawing near to God is good for me; I have made the Lord my refuge, so that I may announce all Thy works."

PAULA

Literal Meaning
LITTLE
Suggested Character Quality or Godly Characteristic
FOLLOWER OF GOD

Suggested Lifetime Scripture Verse — Psalm 73:28
*"But as for me, drawing near to God is good for me; I
have made the Lord my refuge, so that I may announce
all Thy works."*

PAULINE

Literal Meaning
LITTLE
Suggested Character Quality or Godly Characteristic
DEPENDENT ON GOD
Suggested Lifetime Scripture Verse — Psalm 73:28
*"But as for me, drawing near to God is good for me; I
have made the Lord my refuge, so that I may announce
all Thy works."*

PEARL

Literal Meaning
"A JEWEL" — Latin
Suggested Character Quality or Godly Characteristic
PURE HEART
Suggested Lifetime Scripture Verse — Psalm 33:1
*"Rejoice, ye righteous, in the Lord; praise becomes the up-
right!"*

Explanation:
A pearl is the symbol of purity.

PEGGY

Literal Meaning
A PEARL
Suggested Character Quality or Godly Characteristic
PRECIOUS ONE
Suggested Lifetime Scripture Verse — Matthew 5:8
"Blessed are the pure in heart, for they shall see God."

PENNY

Literal Meaning
"WEAVER" — Greek
Suggested Character Quality or Godly Characteristic
CREATIVE SPIRIT

P

Suggested Lifetime Scripture Verse — Psalm 51:10
"Create in me a clean heart, O God, and renew a steadfast spirit within me."

Explanation:
One who weaves creates.

PETE

Literal Meaning
ROCK
Suggested Character Quality or Godly Characteristic
STRONG IN SPIRIT
Suggested Lifetime Scripture Verse — Psalm 27:14
"Wait for the Lord; take courage, and He will give strength to your heart; yes, wait for the Lord."

PETER

Literal Meaning
ROCK
Suggested Character Quality or Godly Characteristic
STRONG IN SPIRIT
Suggested Lifetime Scripture Verse — Psalm 27:14
"Wait for the Lord, take courage, and He will give strength to your heart; yes, wait for the Lord."

PHIL

Literal Meaning
LOVER OF HORSES
Suggested Character Quality or Godly Characteristic
STRONG IN SPIRIT
Suggested Lifetime Scripture Verse — Matthew 6:33
"But you, seek first His kingdom and His righteousness and all these things will be added to you."

Explanation:
See Philip

PHILIP

Literal Meaning
LOVER OF HORSES

Suggested Character Quality or Godly Characteristic
STRONG IN SPIRIT
Suggested Lifetime Scripture Verse — Matthew 6:33
"*But you, seek first His kingdom and His righteousness and all these things will be added to you.*"

Explanation:
The quality of being able to make good sound judgment is characterized by a lover of horses.

PHILLIP

Literal Meaning
LOVER OF HORSES
Suggested Character Quality or Godly Characteristic
STRONG IN SPIRIT
Suggested Lifetime Scripture Verse — Matthew 6:33
"*But you, seek first His kingdom and His righteousness and all these things eill be added to you.*"

Explanation:
See Philip

PHYLLIS

Literal Meaning
LEAF
Suggested Character Quality or Godly Characteristic
TENDERHEARTED
Suggested Lifetime Scripture Verse — Psalm 116:1
"*I love the Lord, for He hears my voice, my supplications.*"

PRISCILLA

Literal Meaning
ANCIENT BIRTH
Suggested Character Quality or Godly Characteristic
FULL OF HONOR
Suggested Lifetime Scripture Verse — Micah 7:7
"*I will wait on the Lord; I will hope in the God of my salvation; my God will hear me.*"

Explanation:
Ancient birth suggests an honorable family.

Q

QUENTIN

Literal Meaning
"FIFTH" — Latin
Suggested Character Quality or Godly Characteristic
A MANLY HEART
Suggested Lifetime Scripture Verse — Psalm 50:23
"He who offers a sacrifice of praise honors Me; to him who prepares his way I will show the salvation of God."

Explanation:
Five is used in Scripture as a symbol of man or humanity; therefore the number five in this case suggests manliness.

QUINN

Literal Meaning
WISE
Suggested Character Quality or Godly Characteristic
FULL OF WISDOM
Suggested Lifetime Scripture Verse — Psalm 111:10
"For reverence of the Lord is the beginning of wisdom. There is insight in all who observe it. His praise is everlasting."

R

RACHAEL

Literal Meaning
LITTLE LAMB
Suggested Character Quality or Godly Characteristic
LITTLE LAMB
Suggested Lifetime Scripture Verse — Isaiah 40:11
"*He will feed His flock like a shepherd; He will gather the lambs in His arms, carrying them in His bosom and gently leading those that are with young.*"

RACHEL

Literal Meaning
LITTLE LAMB
Suggested Character Quality or Godly Characteristic
LITTLE LAMB
Suggested Lifetime Scripture Verse — Isaiah 40:11
"*He will feed His flock like a shepherd; He will gather the lambs in His arms, carrying them in His bosom and gently leading those that are with young.*"

RALPH

Literal Meaning
WOLF-COUNSEL
Suggested Character Quality or Godly Characteristic
BRAVE ADVISOR
Suggested Lifetime Scripture Verse — Proverbs 27:9
"*Oil and perfume make the heart rejoice, as does the pleasantness of a friend's suggestions from the heart.*"

R

RANAE

Literal Meaning
BORN AGAIN
Suggested Character Quality or Godly Characteristic
OF TRANSFORMED HEART
Suggested Lifetime Scripture Verse — Jeremiah 29:13
*"You will seek Me and find Me when you will seek Me
with all your heart."*

RANDAL

Literal Meaning
SHIELD-WOLF
Suggested Character Quality or Godly Characteristic
LOYAL ONE
Suggested Lifetime Scripture Verse — Psalm 116:2
*"Because He has inclined His ear to me, therefore, I will
call on Him as I live."*

RANDALPH

Literal Meaning
"SHIELD-WOLF" — Anglo-saxon
Suggested Character Quality or Godly Characteristic
LOYAL ONE
Suggested Lifetime Scripture Verse — Psalm 116:2
*"Because He has inclined His ear to me, therefore I will call
on Him as long as I live."*

RANDY

Literal Meaning
SHIELD-WOLF
Suggested Character Quality or Godly Characteristic
LOYAL ONE
Suggested Lifetime Scripture Verse — Psalm 116:2
*"Because He has inclined His ear to me, therefore I will
call on Him as long as I live."*

RAY

Literal Meaning
"MIGHTY OR WISE PROTECTOR" — Germanic
Suggested Character Quality or Godly Characteristic
WISE PROTECTOR
Suggested Lifetime Scripture Verse — Psalm 28:7
"*The Lord is my defense and my shield; my heart trusted in Him, and I am helped. Therefore, my heart rejoices, and with my song I will praise Him.*"

RAYMOND

Literal Meaning
COUNSEL-PROTECTION
Suggested Character Quality or Godly Characteristic
MIGHTY
Suggested Lifetime Scripture Verse — Psalm 28:7
"*The Lord is my strength and my shield; my heart trusted in Him, and I am helped. Therefore, my heart rejoices, and with my song I will praise Him.*"

RAYNOLD

Literal Meaning
COUNSEL-PROTECTION
Suggested Character Quality or Godly Characteristic
MIGHTY, POWERFUL
Suggested Lifetime Scripture Verse — Colossians 4:2
"*Keep persevering in prayer; attend to it diligently with the offering of thanks.*"

REBECCA

Literal Meaning
YOKE
Suggested Character Quality or Godly Characteristic
EARNEST DEVOTEE
Suggested Lifetime Scripture Verse — Psalm 73:28
"*But as for me, drawing near to God is good for me; I have made the Lord my refuge, so that I may announce all Thy works.*"

R

REBEKAH

Literal Meaning
YOKE
Suggested Character Quality or Godly Characteristic
DEVOTED ONE
Suggested Lifetime Scripture Verse — Psalm 73:28
"But as for me, drawing near to God is good for me; I have made the Lord my refuge, so that I may announce all Thy works."

REG

Literal Meaning
POWER-MIGHT
Suggested Character Quality or Godly Characteristic
COURAGEOUS
Suggested Lifetime Scripture Verse — Isaiah 12:2
"Behold, God is my salvation; I will trust and not be afraid, for Jehovah, the Lord, is my strength and my song; yes, He has become my salvation."

REGINALD

Literal Meaning
"POWER-MIGHT" — Germanic
Suggested Character Quality or Godly Characteristic
COURAGEOUS
Suggested Lifetime Scripture Verse — Isaiah 12:2
"Behold, God is my salvation; I will trust and not be afraid, for Jehovah, the Lord, is my strength and my song; yes, He has become my salvation."

REID

Literal Meaning
RED
Suggested Character Quality or Godly Characteristic
COURAGEOUS
Suggested Lifetime Scripture Verse — I Corinthians 16:13
"Be alert; stand firm in the faith; play the man; be strong."

Explanation:
The color red associated with a man's name gives the impression of boldness and courage.

RENEE

Literal Meaning
BORN AGAIN
Suggested Character Quality or Godly Characteristic
BORN ANEW
Suggested Lifetime Scripture Verse — Psalm 119:174
"I long for Thy salvation, O Lord; Thy law is my delight."

RETTA

Literal Meaning
THE TYPE OF PERFECT WOMAN
Suggested Character Quality or Godly Characteristic
INDUSTRIOUS
Suggested Lifetime Scripture Verse — Proverbs 31:27
"She looks well to the ways of her household and eats no bread of idleness."

REYNOLD

Literal Meaning
MIGHTY AND POWERFUL
Suggested Character Quality or Godly Characteristic
MIGHTY AND POWERFUL
Suggested Lifetime Scripture Verse — Colossians 4:2
"Keep persevering in prayer; attend to it diligently with the offering of thanks."

REX

Literal Meaning
KING
Suggested Character Quality or Godly Characteristic
MAN OF AUTHORITY
Suggested Lifetime Scripture Verse — Job 17:9
"Yet the righteous will maintain his way, and he who has clean hands will grow stronger."

RHODA

Literal Meaning
A ROSE
Suggested Character Quality or Godly Characteristic

R

FRAGRANT SPIRIT
Suggested Lifetime Scripture Verse — Psalm 54:6
"With a freewill offering I will sacrifice to Thee; I will praise Thy name O Lord, for it is good."

RHONDA

Literal Meaning
GRAND
Suggested Character Quality or Godly Characteristic
STRENGTH OF CHARACTER
Suggested Lifetime Scripture Verse — Proverbs 31:30-31
"Charm is deceitful and beauty is passing, but a woman who reveres the Lord will be praised. Acknowledge the product of her hands; let her works praise her in the gates."

RICHARD

Literal Meaning
POWERFUL RULER
Suggested Character Quality or Godly Characteristic
BRAVE
Suggested Lifetime Scripture Verse — II Timothy 1:7
"For God has not given us a spirit of cowardice, but of power and love and self-control."

RICKY

Literal Meaning
POWERFUL RULER
Suggested Character Quality or Godly Characteristic
BRAVE
Suggested Lifetime Scripture Verse — II Timothy 1:7
"For God has not given us a spirit of cowardice, but of power and love and self-control."

RITA

Literal Meaning
A PEARL
Suggested Character Quality or Godly Characteristic
A PEARL
Suggested Lifetime Scripture Verse — Matthew 5:8
"Blessed are the pure in heart, for they shall see God."

ROANNA

Literal Meaning
GRACIOUS ROSE
Suggested Character Quality or Godly Characteristic
INNER BEAUTY
Suggested Lifetime Scripture Verse — Psalm 29:2
"Ascribe to the Lord the glory of His name; worship the Lord in sacred adornment."

ROBERT

Literal Meaning
SHINING WITH FAME
Suggested Character Quality or Godly Characteristic
EXCELLENT WORTH
Suggested Lifetime Scripture Verse — Psalm 24:3, 4
"Who shall go up into the mountain of the Lord; who shall stand in His holy place? He who has clean hands and a pure heart, who has not lifted up his soul to falsehood, who has not sworn deceptively."

ROBERTA

Literal Meaning
SHINING WITH FAME
Suggested Character Quality or Godly Characteristic
EXCELLENT WORTH
Suggested Lifetime Scripture Verse — Philippians 4:13
"I have strength for every situation through Him who empowers me."

ROBYN

Literal Meaning
SHINING WITH FAME
Suggested Character Quality or Godly Characteristic
STRENGTH OF CHARACTER
Suggested Lifetime Scripture Verse — Philippians 4:13
"I have strength for every situation through Him who empowers me."

R

ROD

Literal Meaning
"FAMOUS RULER" — Germanic
Suggested Character Quality or Godly Characteristic
ESTEEMED ONE
Suggested Lifetime Scripture Verse — Psalm 112:6
"Such a man will never be laid low, for the just shall be held in remembrance forever."

RODNEY

Literal Meaning
FAMOUS ONE'S ISLAND
Suggested Character Quality or Godly Characteristic
ESTEEMED ONE
Suggested Lifetime Scripture Verse — Psalm 112:6
"Such a man will never be laid low, for the just shall be held in remembrance forever."

ROGER

Literal Meaning
FAMOUS SPEARMAN
Suggested Character Quality or Godly Characteristic
GOD'S WARRIOR
Suggested Lifetime Scripture Verse — II Corinthians 10:4
"For the weapons of our warfare are not physical, but they are powerful with God's help for the tearing down of fortresses."

ROLF

Literal Meaning
FAME-WOLF
Suggested Character Quality or Godly Characteristic
STRONG; MANLY
Suggested Lifetime Scripture Verse — Joshua 1:9
"Have I not commanded you? Be resolute and strong! Be not afraid, and be not dismayed; for the Lord your God is with you everywhere you go."

ROLLIN

Literal Meaning
FROM THE FAMOUS LAND
Suggested Character Quality or Godly Characteristic
STRONG; MANLY
Suggested Lifetime Scripture Verse — Philippians 4:13
"I have strength for every situation through Him who empowers me."

RON

Literal Meaning
MIGHTY POWER
Suggested Character Quality or Godly Characteristic
STRONG ONE
Suggested Lifetime Scripture Verse — Ephesians 6:10
"In conclusion, be strong in the Lord and in the strength of His might."

RONALD

Literal Meaning
MIGHTY POWER
Suggested Character Quality or Godly Characteristic
MIGHTY POWER
Suggested Lifetime Scripture Verse — Ephesians 6:10
"In conclusion, be strong in the Lord and in the strength of His might."

RONDA

Literal Meaning
GRAND
Suggested Character Quality or Godly Characteristic
STRENGTH OF CHARACTER
Suggested Lifetime Scripture Verse — Proverbs 31:30-31
"Charm is deceitful, and beauty is vain, but a woman who fears the Lord is to be praised. Give her the fruit of her hands, and let her works praise her in the gates."

ROSA

Literal Meaning
ROSE

R

Suggested Character Quality or Godly Characteristic
GIVER OF LOVE
Suggested Lifetime Scripture Verse — I Corinthians 13:13
"*There remain then, faith, hope, love, these three; but the greatest of these is love.*"

ROSALIE

Literal Meaning
A ROSE
Suggested Character Quality or Godly Characteristic
GIVER OF LOVE
Suggested Lifetime Scripture Verse — I Corinthians 13:13
"*There remain then, faith, hope, love, these three; but the greatest of these is love.*"

ROSAMOND

Literal Meaning
ROSE
Suggested Character Quality or Godly Characteristic
GIVER OF LOVE
Suggested Lifetime Scripture Verse — I Corinthians 13:13
"*There remain then faith, hope, love, these three; but the greatest of these is love.*"

ROSANNE

Literal Meaning
ROSANNE
Suggested Character Quality or Godly Characteristic
GIVER OF LOVE
Suggested Lifetime Scripture Verse — I Corinthians 13:13
"*There remain then, faith, hope, love, these three; but the greatest of these is love.*"

ROSE

Literal Meaning
A ROSE
Suggested Character Quality or Godly Character
GIVER OF LOVE
Suggested Lifetime Scripture Verse — I Corinthians 13:13
"*There remain then, faith, hope, love, these three; but the greatest of these is love.*"

ROSEMARIE

Literal Meaning
THE ROSE OF ST. MARY
Suggested Character Quality or Godly Characteristic
GIVER OF LOVE
Suggested Lifetime Scripture Verse — I Corinthians 13:13
"There remain then, faith, hope, love, these three; but the greatest of these is love."

ROSEMARY

Literal Meaning
ROSE OF ST. MARY
Suggested Character Quality or Godly Characteristic
GIVER OF LOVE
Suggested Lifetime Scripture Verse — I Corinthians 13:13
"There remain then, faith, hope, love, these three; but the greatest of these is love."

ROSETTE

Literal Meaning
ROSE
Suggested Character Quality or Godly Characteristic
COMPASSIONATE SPIRIT
Suggested Lifetime Scripture Verse — I Corinthians 13:13
"There remain then, faith, hope, love, these three; but the greatest of these is love."

ROSS

Literal Meaning
FROM THE PENINSULA
Suggested Character Quality or Godly Characteristic
GALLANT
Suggested Lifetime Scripture Verse — Psalm 27:14
"Wait for the Lord; take courage, and He will give strength to your heart; yes, wait for the Lord."

ROXANNE

Literal Meaning
BRILLIANT ONE

R

Suggested Character Quality or Godly Characteristic
COMING WITH LIGHT
Suggested Lifetime Scripture Verse — Psalm 27:1
"The Lord is my light and my salvation; whom shall I fear?
The Lord is the stronghold of my life; of whom shall I be
afraid."

ROY

Literal Meaning
KINGLY
Suggested Character Quality or Godly Characteristic
GRACIOUS; MANLY
Suggested Lifetime Scripture Verse — Jeremiah 17:7
"Blessed is the man who trusts in the Lord, whose trust
is the Lord."

Explanation:
These qualities characterize a kingly man.

RUBY

Literal Meaning
RED JEWEL
Suggested Character Quality or Godly Characteristic
EXCELLENT SPIRIT
Suggested Lifetime Scripture Verse — Psalm 7:8
". . . May the Lord judge the people. Vindicate me, O Lord,
according to my righteousness and according to the integrity
that is upon me."

Explanation:
A jewel must have excellent qualities to be considered
precious.

RUDOLPH

Literal Meaning
FAMOUS WOLF
Suggested Character Quality or Godly Characteristic
LOYAL ONE
Suggested Lifetime Scripture Verse — Psalm 116:2
"Because He has inclined His ear to me, therefore I will
call on Him as long as I live."

RUSSELL

Literal Meaning
RED-HAIRED ONE
Suggested Character Quality or Godly Characteristic
WISE DISCRETION
Suggested Lifetime Scripture Verse — Isaiah 28:26
"*His God correctly instructs and teaches him.*"

RUTH

Literal Meaning
COMPASSIONATE, BEAUTIFUL
Suggested Character Quality or Godly Characteristic
COMPASSIONATE
Suggested Lifetime Scripture Verse — Proverbs 31:20
"*She opens her palm to the poor and reaches out her hands to the needy.*"

RYAN

Literal Meaning
LITTLE KING
Suggested Character Quality or Godly Characteristic
MAN OF DISTINCTION
Suggested Lifetime Scripture Verse — Psalm 112:5
"*It is well with him who is generous and ready to lend, the man who conducts his business with fairness.*"

S

SALLY

Literal Meaning
PRINCESS
Suggested Character Quality or Godly Characteristic
GOD'S PRINCESS
Suggested Lifetime Scripture Verse — I Peter 2:9
"But you are a chosen race, a royal priesthood, a holy nation, a people of His acquisition, so that you may proclaim the perfections of Him who called you out of darkness into His marvelous light."

SAMUEL

Literal Meaning
HIS NAME IS GOD—HEARD OR ASKED OF GOD
Suggested Character Quality or Godly Characteristic
INTEGRITY
Suggested Lifetime Scripture Verse — Proverbs 21:3
"To practice righteousness and justice is more acceptable to the Lord than sacrifice."

SANDRA

Literal Meaning
HELPER; DEFENDER OF MANKIND
Suggested Character Quality or Godly Characteristic
COMPASSION WITH HUMILITY
Suggested Lifetime Scripture Verse — Proverbs 31:20
"She opens her palm to the poor and reaches out her hands to the needy."

SARA

Literal Meaning
PRINCESS
Suggested Character Quality or Godly Characteristic
GOD'S PRINCESS
Suggested Lifetime Scripture Verse — I Peter 2:9
"But you are a chosen race, a royal priesthood, a holy nation, a people of His acquisition, so that you may proclaim the perfection of Him who called you out of darkness into His marvelous light."

SARAH

Literal Meaning
PRINCESS
Suggested Character Quality or Godly Characteristic
GOD'S PRINCESS
Suggested Lifetime Scripture Verse — I Peter 2:9
"But you are a chosen race, a royal priesthood, a holy nation, a people of His acquisition, so that you may proclaim the perfections of Him who called you out of darkness into His marvelous light."

SCOTT

Literal Meaning
FROM SCOTLAND
Suggested Character Quality or Godly Characteristic
LOYAL
Suggested Lifetime Scripture Verse — Romans 12:9-10
"Let your love be sincere, clinging to the right with abhorrence of evil. Be joined together in a brotherhood of mutual love, trying to outdo one another in showing respect."

SEAN

Literal Meaning
GOD IS GRACIOUS
Suggested Character Quality or Godly Characteristic
GOD'S GIFT
Suggested Lifetime Scripture Verse — Isaiah 43:10
"You are My witness, says the Lord, and My servant whom I have chosen, in order that you may know and believe

S

Me, and understand that I am He. Before Me no God was formed, nor shall there be after Me."

SELMER

Literal Meaning
NO LITERAL MEANING FOUND
Suggested Character Quality or Godly Characteristic
STRONG IN FAITH
Suggested Lifetime Scripture Verse — Habakkuk 3:18
"Yet I will rejoice in the Lord, I will joy in the God of my salvation."

SHANNON

Literal Meaning
LITTLE-WISE ONE
Suggested Character Quality or Godly Characteristic
GRACIOUS SPIRIT
Suggested Lifetime Scripture Verse — Psalm 84:11
"For the Lord God is a sun and shield, the Lord bestows mercy and honor. He holds back nothing good from those who walk uprightly."

SHARON

Literal Meaning
A PRINCESS
Suggested Character Quality or Godly Characteristic
A PRINCESS
Suggested Lifetime Scripture Verse — I Peter 2:9
"But you are a chosen race, a royal priesthood, a holy nation, a people of His acquisition, so that you may proclaim the perfections of Him who called you out of darkness into His light."

SHAWN

Literal Meaning
JEHOVAH HAS BEEN GRACIOUS
Suggested Character Quality or Godly Characteristic
GOD'S GIFT
Suggested Lifetime Scripture Verse — Isaiah 43:10

"You are My witnesses, says the Lord, and My servant whom I have chosen, in order that you may know and believe Me, and understand that I am He. Before Me no God was formed, nor shall there be after Me."

SHEILA

Literal Meaning
IRISH HEAVENLY
Suggested Character Quality or Godly Characteristic
CONTENTED HEART
Suggested Lifetime Scripture Verse — Psalm 18:28
"For Thou causest my lamp to shine; the Lord, my God, illumines my darkness."

SHELBY

Literal Meaning
FROM THE LEDGE ESTATE
Suggested Character Quality or Godly Characteristic
WHERE GOD DWELLS
Suggested Lifetime Scripture Verse — Jeremiah 7:7
"Then I will let you dwell in this place, in the land that I gave to your fathers forever."

SHELLEY

Literal Meaning
FROM THE MEADOW ON THE LEDGE
Suggested Character Quality or Godly Characteristic
PROTECTOR OF LIFE
Suggested Lifetime Scripture Verse — Psalm 23:1-2
"The Lord is my Shepherd, I shall not lack; He makes me to lie down in green pastures."

SHELLY

Literal Meaning
SHELL ISLAND
Suggested Character Quality or Godly Characteristic
PEACEFUL SPIRIT
Suggested Lifetime Scripture Verse — Psalm 23:1-2
"The Lord is my shepherd; I shall not lack; He makes me to lie down in green pastures."

S

SHERI

Literal Meaning
LITTLE WOMANLY ONE
Suggested Character Quality or Godly Characteristic
CHERISHED ONE
Suggested Lifetime Scripture Verse — Zephaniah 3:17
"The Lord, your God, is in your midst, a Mighty One who will save. He will rejoice over you with delight; He will rest you in His love; He will be joyful over you with singing."

SHERMAN

Literal Meaning
CLOTH-CUTTER
Suggested Character Quality or Godly Characteristic
INDUSTRIOUS
Suggested Lifetime Scripture Verse — Matthew 5:16
"Similarly let your light shine for everyone in the house."

SHERRI

Literal Meaning
LITTLE WOMANLY ONE
Suggested Character Quality or Godly Characteristic
CHERISHED ONE
Suggested Lifetime Scripture Verse — Zephaniah 3:17
"The Lord, your God, is in your midst, a Mighty One who will save. He will rejoice over you with delight; He will rest you in His love; He will be joyful over you with singing."

SHERRY

Literal Meaning
LITTLE WOMANLY ONE
Suggested Character Quality or Godly Characteristic
CHERISHED ONE
Suggested Lifetime Scripture Verse — Zephaniah 3:17
"The Lord, your God, is in your midst, a Mighty One who will save. He will rejoice over you with delight; He will rest you in His love; He will be joyful over you with singing."

SHIRLEY

Literal Meaning
FROM THE BRIGHT MEADOW

Suggested Character Quality or Godly Characteristic
RESTFUL SPIRIT
Suggested Lifetime Scripture Verse — Isaiah 26:4
"*Trust in the Lord forever, for the Lord God is the Rock of Ages.*"

SIDNEY

Literal Meaning
"SAINT DENIS" — Form of French
Suggested Character Quality or Godly Characteristic
DISCERNER OF EXCELLENCE
Suggested Lifetime Scripture Verse — Matthew 6:33
"*But you, seek first His kingdom and His righteousness and all these things will be added to you.*"

Explanation:
Taken from the meaning for Dennis

SIMON

Literal Meaning
HEARING
Suggested Character Quality or Godly Characteristic
OBEDIENT SPIRIT
Suggested Lifetime Scripture Verse — Psalm 37:5
"*Commit your way to the Lord; trust in Him, too, and He will bring it about.*"

SIMONE

Literal Meaning
HEARER; ONE WHO HEARS
Suggested Character Quality or Godly Characteristic
OBEDIENT SPIRIT
Suggested Lifetime Scripture Verse — Psalm 37:5
"*Commit your way to the Lord; trust in Him, too, and He will bring it about.*"

SOPHIA

Literal Meaning
WISE
Suggested Character Quality or Godly Character

S

WOMAN OF WISDOM
Suggested Lifetime Scripture Verse — Proverbs 2:6
"*For the Lord gives wisdom; from His mouth come knowledge and discernment.*"

SONJA

Literal Meaning
WISDOM
Suggested Character Quality or Godly Characteristic
WOMAN OF WISDOM
Suggested Lifetime Scripture Verse — Proverbs 2:6
"*For the Lord gives wisdom; from His mouth come knowledge and discernment.*"

SONJIA

Literal Meaning
WISDOM
Suggested Character Quality or Godly Characteristic
WOMAN OF WISDOM
Suggested Lifetime Scripture Verse — Proverbs 2:6
"*For the Lord gives wisdom; from His mouth come knowledge and discernment.*"

SONYA

Literal Meaning
WISE
Suggested Character Quality or Godly Characteristic
WOMAN OF WISDOM
Suggested Lifetime Scripture Verse — Proverbs 2:6
"*For the Lord gives wisdom; from His mouth come knowledge and discernment.*"

SPENCER

Literal Meaning
DISPENSER OF PROVISIONS
Suggested Character Quality or Godly Characteristic
FAITHFUL STEWARD
Suggested Lifetime Scripture Verse — Deuteronomy 11:1

"Love the Lord your God, therefore, and always heed His charge, His laws, His ordinances, and His commandments. Of the Lord your God's discipline you must be ever mindful."

STACIE

Literal Meaning
OF THE RESURRECTION
Suggested Character Quality or Godly Characteristic
TRANSFORMED HEART
Suggested Lifetime Scripture Verse — Psalm 11:7
"For the Lord is righteous; He loves acts of righteousness; His countenance beholds the upright."

STACEY

Literal Meaning
OF THE RESURRECTION
Suggested Character Quality or Godly Characteristic
TRANSFORMED HEART
Suggested Lifetime Scripture Verse — Psalm 11:7
"For the Lord is righteous; He loves acts of righteousness; His countenance beholds the upright."

STACY

Literal Meaning
OF THE RESURRECTION
Suggested Character Quality or Godly Characteristic
TRANSFORMED HEART
Suggested Lifetime Scripture Verse — Psalm 11:7
"For the Lord is righteous; He loves acts of righteousness; His countenance beholds the upright."

STAN

Literal Meaning
DWELLER AT THE ROCKY MEADOW
Suggested Character Quality or Godly Characteristic
STURDY SPIRIT
Suggested Lifetime Scripture Verse — Micah 6:8
"He has declared to you, O man, what is good, and what does the Lord require of you but to do justice, to love mercy, and to walk humbly with your God."

S

Explanation:
See Stanley

STANLEY

Literal Meaning
DWELLER AT THE ROCKY MEADOW
Suggested Character Quality or Godly Characteristic
STURDY SPIRIT
Suggested Lifetime Scripture Verse — Micah 6:8
"*He has declared to you, O man, what is good, and what does the Lord require of you but to do justice, to love mercy, and to walk humbly with your God.*"

Explanation:
A rocky meadow suggests that one would need a sturdy, steadfast spirit in order to survive.

STELLA

Literal Meaning
"A STAR" — Latin
Suggested Character Quality or Godly Characteristic
WOMAN OF ESTEEM
Suggested Lifetime Scripture Verse — Proverbs 2:6
"*For the Lord gives wisdom; from His mouth come knowledge and discernment.*"

STEPHANIE

Literal Meaning
CROWNED ONE
Suggested Character Quality or Godly Characteristic
CROWNED ONE
Suggested Lifetime Scripture Verse — Isaiah 58:14
"*Then you shall find your delight in the Lord, and I will make you ride on the highways of the earth; I will nourish you with the heritage of Jacob, your father, for the mouth of the Lord has spoken it.*"

STEPHEN

Literal Meaning
CROWNED ONE

Suggested Character Quality or Godly Characteristic
CROWNED ONE
Suggested Lifetime Scripture Verse — Psalm 103:2, 4
*"Bless the Lord, O my soul, and forget none of His benefits
. . . Who redeems your life from the grave, who crowns you
with lovingkindness and mercy."*

STERLING

Literal Meaning
STANDARD OF EXCELLENT QUALITY
Suggested Character Quality or Godly Characteristic
EXCELLENT CHARACTER
Suggested Lifetime Scripture Verse — Job 23:10
*"But He knows the way which I take, and when He has
tested me I shall come forth as gold."*

STEVE

Literal Meaning
CROWNED ONE
Suggested Character Quality or Godly Characteristic
CROWNED ONE
Suggested Lifetime Scripture Verse — Psalm 103:2; 4
*"Bless the Lord, O my soul, and forget none of His benefits
. . . Who redeems your life from the grave, who crowns you
with lovingkindness and mercy."*

STEVEN

Literal Meaning
CROWNED ONE
Suggested Character Quality or Godly Characteristic
CROWNED ONE
Suggested Lifetime Scripture Verse — Psalm 103:2, 4
*"Bless the Lord, O my soul, and forget none of His benefits
. . . Who redeems your life from the grave, who crowns you
with lovingkindness and mercy."*

STUART

Literal Meaning
"CARETAKER" — Anglo-Saxon

S

Suggested Character Quality or Godly Characteristic
HELPFUL SPIRIT
Suggested Lifetime Scripture Verse — Romans 15:14
"I myself am convinced about you, my brothers, that you are full of goodness, amply furnished with knowledge, and competent to advise one another."

SUE

Literal Meaning
LILY OR GRACEFUL LILY
Suggested Character Quality or Godly Characteristic
FULL OF GRACE
Suggested Lifetime Scripture Verse — Psalm 84:11
"For the Lord God is a sun and shield; the Lord bestows mercy and honor. He holds back nothing good from those who walk uprightly."

SUSAN

Literal Meaning
LILY OR GRACEFUL LILY
Suggested Character Quality or Godly Characteristic
FULL OF GRACE
Suggested Lifetime Scripture Verse — Psalm 84:11
"For the Lord God is a sun and shield; the Lord bestows mercy and honor. He holds back nothing good from those who walk uprightly."

SUZANNE

Literal Meaning
LILY OR GRACEFUL
Suggested Character Quality or Godly Characteristic
PURE IN GRACE
Suggested Lifetime Scripture Verse — Psalm 84:11
"For the Lord is a sun and shield; the Lord bestows mercy and honor. He holds back nothing good from those who walk uprightly."

SYLVIA

Literal Meaning
FROM THE FOREST

Suggested Character Quality or Godly Characteristic
SECURE ONE
Suggested Lifetime Scripture Verse — Job 11:18
"You will feel confident, because you have hoped you will look around and lie down without fear."

T

TAMMY

Literal Meaning
A TWIN
Suggested Character Quality or Godly Characteristic
SEEKER OF TRUTH
Suggested Lifetime Scripture Verse — Psalm 63:1
"O God, Thou art my God, I seek Thee earnestly; my soul thirsts for Thee, my flesh longs for Thee in a dry and worn-out land, where there is no water."

TANIA

Literal Meaning
A FAIRY QUEEN
Suggested Character Quality or Godly Characteristic
NOBLE SPIRIT
Suggested Lifetime Scripture Verse — Proverbs 31:31
"Acknowledge the product of her hands; let her works praise her in the gates."

TED

Literal Meaning
GIFT OF GOD
Suggested Character Quality or Godly Characteristic
GIFT OF GOD
Suggested Lifetime Scripture Verse — Isaiah 43:10
"You are my witnesses, says the Lord, and My servant whom I have chosen, in order that you may know and believe Me, and understand that I am He. Before Me no God was formed, nor shall there be after Me."

TERESA

Literal Meaning
REAPER
Suggested Character Quality or Godly Characteristic
INDUSTRIOUS
Suggested Lifetime Scripture Verse — Psalm 18:32
"The God who girds me with strength, and makes my way perfect."

TERRENCE

Literal Meaning
SMOOTH-POLISHED ONE
Suggested Character Quality or Godly Characteristic
SMOOTH-POLISHED ONE
Suggested Lifetime Scripture Verse — Philippians 1:6
"Of this I am convinced, that He who has begun a good work in you will bring it to completion in the day of Christ Jesus."

TERRI (F)

Literal Meaning
REAPER
Suggested Character Quality or Godly Characteristic
CARING ONE
Suggested Lifetime Scripture Verse — Jude 1:21
"Keep yourselves in the Love of God, all the while awaiting the mercy of our Lord Jesus Christ for eternal life."

TERRI (M)

Literal Meaning
SMOOTH-POLISHED ONE
Suggested Character Quality or Godly Characteristic
SMOOTH-POLISHED ONE
Suggested Lifetime Scripture Verse — Philippians 1:6
"Of this I am convinced, that He who has begun a good work in you will bring it to completion in the day of Christ Jesus."

T

TERRY

Literal Meaning
SMOOTH-POLISHED ONE
Suggested Character Quality or Godly Characteristic
SMOOTH-POLISHED ONE
Suggested Lifetime Scripture Verse — Philippians 1:6
"*Of this I am convinced, that He who has begun a good work in you will bring it to completion in the day of Jesus Christ.*"

THELMA

Literal Meaning
NURSING
Suggested Character Quality or Godly Characteristic
TRUSTFUL HEART
Suggested Lifetime Scripture Verse — Isaiah 30:15
"*For thus said the Lord God, the Holy One of Israel. In returning and resting you shall be saved; in quietness and in trust shall be your strength.*"

THEODORE

Literal Meaning
GIFT OF GOD
Suggested Character Quality or Godly Characteristic
GIFT OF GOD
Suggested Lifetime Scripture Verse — Isaiah 43:10
"*You are My witnesses, says the Lord, and My servant whom I have chosen, in order that you may know and believe Me, and understand that I am He. Before me no God was formed, nor shall there be after Me.*"

THERESA

Literal Meaning
REAPER
Suggested Character Quality or Godly Characteristic
INDUSTRIOUS
Suggested Lifetime Scripture Verse — Psalm 18:32
"*The God who girds me with strength, and makes my way perfect.*"

TIFFANY

Literal Meaning
APPEARANCE OF GOD
Suggested Character Quality or Godly Characteristic
IN GOD'S IMAGE
Suggested Lifetime Scripture Verse — Psalm 37:6
"*He will bring forth your righteousness like the light, and your life as the noonday brightness.*"

TIM

Literal Meaning
HONORING GOD
Suggested Character Quality or Godly Characteristic
HONORING GOD
Suggested Lifetime Scripture Verse — Psalm 104:1
"*Bless the Lord, O my soul! O Lord my God, Thou are very great! Thou art clothed with honor and majesty.*"

TINA

Literal Meaning
No Literal Meaning Found
Suggested Character Quality or Godly Characteristic
OBEDIENT HEART
Suggested Lifetime Scripture Verse — Psalm 18:22
"*For all His ordinances were before me, and His statutes I did not put away form me.*"

Explanation:
Since this name has no real meaning of its own a combination of meanings from Christina and Ernestina was used.

THOMAS

Literal Meaning
A TWIN
Suggested Character Quality or Godly Characteristic
SEEKER OF TRUTH
Suggested Lifetime Scripture Verse — Psalm 63:1
"*O God, Thou art my God, I seek Thee earnestly; my soul thirsts for Thee in a dry and worn-out land, where there is no water.*"

T

Explanation:
The character quality of this name applies to the disciple Thomas. He had to seek truth out himself.

TIMOTHY

Literal Meaning
HONORING GOD
Suggested Character Quality or Godly Characteristic
HONORING GOD
Suggested Lifetime Scripture Verse — Psalm 104:1
"*Bless the Lord, O my soul! O Lord my God, Thou art very great! Thou art clothed with honor and majesty.*"

TODD

Literal Meaning
A FOX
Suggested Character Quality or Godly Characteristic
WISE CHOOSER
Suggested Lifetime Scripture Verse — Proverbs 3:5-6
"*Trust in the Lord with all your heart and lean not on your own understanding; in all your ways acknowledge Him, and He will direct your paths.*"

TOM

Literal Meaning
A TWIN
Suggested Character Quality or Godly Characteristic
SEEKER OF TRUTH
Suggested Lifetime Scripture Verse — Psalm 63:1
"*O God, Thou art my God, I seek Thee earnestly; my soul thirsts for Thee; my flesh longs for Thee in a dry and worn-out land, where there is no water.*"

Explanation:
See Thomas

TONY

Literal Meaning
INESTIMABLE
Suggested Character Quality or Godly Characteristic
PRICELESS ONE

Suggested Lifetime Scripture Verse — Psalm 21:6
"*Yes, forever Thou dost make him most blessed; Thou dost delight him with joy by Thy presence.*"

TRACEY

Literal Meaning
TO REAP
Suggested Character Quality or Godly Characteristic
INDUSTRIOUS
Suggested Lifetime Scripture Verse — Proverbs 31:27
"*She looks well to the ways of her household and eats no bread of idleness.*"

TRACY (F)

Literal Meaning
TO REAP
Suggested Character Quality or Godly Characteristic
INDUSTRIOUS
Suggested Lifetime Scripture Verse — Proverbs 31:27
"*She looks well to the ways of her household and eats no bread of idleness.*"

TRACY (M)

Literal Meaning
TO REAP
Suggested Character Quality or Godly Characteristic
INDUSTRIOUS
Suggested Lifetime Scripture Verse — Ephesians 6:10
"*In conclusion, be strong in the Lord and in the strength of His might.*"

TRAVIS

Literal Meaning
FROM THE CROSSROADS
Suggested Character Quality or Godly Characteristic
DILIGENT SPIRIT
Suggested Lifetime Scripture Verse — Proverbs 24:5
"*A wise man is strong, and a man of knowledge adds to his strength.*"

T

TRISHA

Literal Meaning
NOBLE ONE
Suggested Character Quality or Godly Characteristic
FULL OF HONOR
Suggested Lifetime Scripture Verse — Psalm 62:7
"*My salvation and my glory depend on God; the rock of my defence, my refuge is in God.*"

TROY

Literal Meaning
AT THE PLACE OF THE CURLY-HAIRED PEOPLE
Suggested Character Quality or Godly Characteristic
RELIABLE
Suggested Lifetime Scripture Verse — Micah 6:8
"*He has declared to you, O man, what is good, and what does the Lord require of you but to do justice, to love mercy and to walk humbly with your God.*"

TYLER

Literal Meaning
Occupational Name
Suggested Character Quality or Godly Characteristic
INDUSTRIOUS ONE
Suggested Lifetime Scripture Verse — Hebrews 13:16
"*Do not forget to do good and be generous, for with such sacrifices God is well pleased.*"

VALERIE

Literal Meaning
"STRONG" — Latin
Suggested Character Quality or Godly Characteristic
OF DETERMINED PURPOSE
Suggested Lifetime Scripture Verse — Psalm 27:14
"Wait for the Lord; take courage, and He will give strength to your heart; yes, wait for the Lord."

VAN

Literal Meaning
THRESHER
Suggested Character Quality or Godly Characteristic
INDUSTRIOUS SPIRIT
Suggested Lifetime Scripture Verse — Psalm 21:6
"Trust in the Lord and do good; inhabit the land and practice faithfulness."

VANESSA

Literal Meaning
No literal meaning found
Suggested Character Quality or Godly Characteristic
WALKS WITH GOD
Suggested Lifetime Scripture Verse — Psalm 37:5
"Commit your way to the Lord; trust in Him, too, and He will bring it about."

VERA

Literal Meaning
FAITH; TRUE
Suggested Character Quality or Godly Characteristic
FAITHFUL SPIRIT

V

Suggested Lifetime Scripture Verse — Psalm 119:124
"*Deal with Thy servant according to Thy lovingkindness, and teach me Thy statutes.*"

VERONICA

Literal Meaning
TRUE IMAGE
Suggested Character Quality or Godly Characteristic
TRUE-HEARTED
Suggested Lifetime Scripture Verse — Psalm 119:132
"*Turn Thou to me and have mercy on me, as is Thy way with those who love Thy name.*"

VERNA

Literal Meaning
SPRING-LIKE
Suggested Character Quality or Godly Characteristic
ABUNDANT LIFE
Suggested Lifetime Scripture Verse — Psalm 52:8
"*But I am like a green olive tree in the house of God; I trust in God's lovingkindness forever and ever.*"

Explanation:
Spring is a time of new and abundant life.

VERNON

Literal Meaning
SPRING-LIKE
Suggested Character Quality or Godly Characteristic
ABUNDANT LIFE
Suggested Lifetime Scripture Verse — Psalm 52:8
"*But I am like a green olive tree in the house of God; I trust in God's lovingkindness forever and ever.*"

Explanation:
See Verna

VICKI

Literal Meaning
VICTORY
Suggested Character Quality or Godly Characteristic

VICTORIOUS SPIRIT
Suggested Lifetime Scripture Verse — Psalm 89:1
"I will sing of the mercies of the Lord forever; I will make known Thy faithfulness with my mouth from generation to generation."

VICTOR

Literal Meaning
CONQUEROR
Suggested Character Quality or Godly Characteristic
VICTORIOUS LIFE
Suggested Lifetime Scripture Verse — I Corinthians 15:57
"But thanks be to God, who gives us the victory through our Lord Jesus Christ!"

VICTORIA

Literal Meaning
VICTORIOUS
Suggested Character Quality or Godly Characteristic
VICTORIOUS SPIRIT
Suggested Lifetime Scripture Verse — Psalm 89:1
"I will sing of the mercies of the Lord forever; I will make known Thy faithfulness with my mouth from generation to generation."

VINCENT

Literal Meaning
CONQUERING ONE
Suggested Character Quality or Godly Characteristic
STRONG IN VICTORY
Suggested Lifetime Scripture Verse — Psalm 118:14
"The Lord is my strength and my song; He has become my salvation."

VIOLET

Literal Meaning
A VIOLET FLOWER
Suggested Character Quality or Godly Characteristic
HUMBLE
Suggested Lifetime Scripture Verse — Isaiah 30:15

V

"For thus says the Lord God, the Holy One of Israel; in conversion and rest you shall be saved; in quietness and confidence shall be your strength."

Explanation:
A violet is considered a humble flower.

VIRGINIA

Literal Meaning
MAIDENLY
Suggested Character Quality or Godly Characteristic
PURE ONE
Suggested Lifetime Scripture Verse — Psalm 119:1
"Blessed are those whose way is upright, who walk in the law of the Lord."

VIVIAN

Literal Meaning
ALIVE
Suggested Character Quality or Godly Characteristic
FULL OF LIFE
Suggested Lifetime Scripture Verse — Psalm 52:8
"But I am like a green olive tree in the house of God; I trust in God's lovingkindness forever and ever."

WADE

Literal Meaning
THE ADVANCER
Suggested Character Quality or Godly Characteristic
CHAMPION
Suggested Lifetime Scripture Verse — Philippians 3:14
*"I push on to the goal for the prize of God's heavenly call
in Christ Jesus."*

WALLACE

Literal Meaning
MAN FROM WALES
Suggested Character Quality or Godly Characteristic
INDUSTRIOUS
Suggested Lifetime Scripture Verse — Matthew 5:16
*"Similarly let your light shine among the people, so that
they observe your good works and give glory to your heavenly
Father."*

WALTER

Literal Meaning
POWERFUL WARRIOR; ARMY RULER
Suggested Character Quality or Godly Characteristic
POWERFUL
Suggested Lifetime Scripture Verse — Philippians 4:13
*"I have strength for every situation through Him who em-
powers me."*

W

WANDA

Literal Meaning
WANDERER
Suggested Character Quality or Godly Characteristic
WALKS WITH GOD
Suggested Lifetime Scripture Verse — Psalm 37:5
"*Commit your way to the Lord; trust in Him, too, and He will bring it about.*"

WARD

Literal Meaning
GUARD
Suggested Character Quality or Godly Characteristic
SECURE SPIRIT
Suggested Lifetime Scripture Verse — Nahum 1:7
"*The Lord is good, a stronghold in the day of trouble; He knows those who commit themselves to Him.*"

Explanation:
A guard provides security.

WARREN

Literal Meaning
PROTECTING FRIEND
Suggested Character Quality or Godly Characteristic
ONE WHO PROTECTS
Suggested Lifetime Scripture Verse — Psalm 11:7
"*For the Lord is righteous; He loves acts of righteousness; His countenance beholds the upright.*"

WAYNE

Literal Meaning
WAGONER OR WAGONMAKER
Suggested Character Quality or Godly Characteristic
LIFTER OF CARES
Suggested Lifetime Scripture Verse — Galatians 6:2
"*Carry one another's burden and thus fulfill the law of Christ.*"

WENDY

Literal Meaning
WANDERER
Suggested Character Quality or Godly Characteristic
WALKS WITH GOD
Suggested Lifetime Scripture Verse — Psalm 37:5
"Commit your way to the Lord; trust in Him, too, and He will bring it about."

WESLEY

Literal Meaning
WEST FIELD
Suggested Character Quality or Godly Characteristic
PROSPEROUS SPIRIT
Suggested Lifetime Scripture Verse — Psalm 13:6
"Let me sing to the Lord because He has dealt generously with me."

Explanation:
Those names which have to do with fields, meadows, or land suggest prosperity.

WHITNEY

Literal Meaning
FROM THE WHITE-HAIRED ONE'S ISLAND
Suggested Character Quality or Godly Characteristic
SEEKER OF WISDOM
Suggested Lifetime Scripture Verse — Psalm 111:10
"For reverence of the Lord is the beginning of wisdom. There is insight in all who observe it. His praise is everlasting."

WILBUR

Literal Meaning
BRIGHT PLEDGE
Suggested Character Quality or Godly Characteristic
NOBLE IN HONOR
Suggested Lifetime Scripture Verse — Psalm 29:1
"Give to the Lord, O you sons of the mighty, give to the Lord glory and strength."

W

WILL

Literal Meaning
OF RESOLUTE WILL
Suggested Character Quality or Godly Characteristic
OF RESOLUTE SPIRIT
Suggested Lifetime Scripture Verse — Psalm 1:2
"But his delight is in the law of the Lord and His law he ponders day and night."

WILLARD

Literal Meaning
RESOLUTE AND BRAVE
Suggested Character Quality or Godly Characteristic
OF RESOLUTE SPIRIT
Suggested Lifetime Scripture Verse — Psalm 1:2
"But his delight is in the law of the Lord and His law he ponders day and night."

WILLIAM

Literal Meaning
RESOLUTE PROTECTOR
Suggested Character Quality or Godly Characteristic
GREAT PROTECTOR
Suggested Lifetime Scripture Verse — Micah 6:8
"And what does the Lord require of you but to do justice, to love mercy and to walk humbly with your God."

WILMA

Literal Meaning
WILL HELMET
Suggested Character Quality or Godly Characteristic
GIVER OF SECURITY
Suggested Lifetime Scripture Verse — Romans 15:13
"So may God, the fountain of hope, fill you with all joy and peace in your believing, so that you may enjoy overflowing hope by the power of the Holy Spirit."

Explanation:
One who guards gives security.

WINIFRED

Literal Meaning
WHITE WAVE
Suggested Character Quality or Godly Characteristic
PURE OF HEART
Suggested Lifetime Scripture Verse — Psalm 119:1
"Blessed are those whose way is upright, who walk in the law of the Lord!"

WINSTON

Literal Meaning
"FRIEND" — Anglo-saxon
Suggested Character Quality or Godly Characteristic
FRIENDLY SPIRIT
Suggested Lifetime Scripture Verse — Proverbs 18:24
"A man has many friends for companionship, but there is a friend who sticks closer than a brother."

Y

YVONNE

Literal Meaning
"HERO" — Anglo-saxon
Suggested Character Quality or Godly Characteristic
COURAGEOUS HEART
Suggested Lifetime Scripture Verse — Psalm 7:10
"My shield depends upon God, who saves the upright in heart."

Z

ZACHARY

Literal Meaning
"JEHOVAH HAS REMEMBERED" — Hebrew
Suggested Character Quality or Godly Characteristic
THE LORD REMEMBERS
Suggested Lifetime Scripture Verse — Psalm 17:7
"In a marvelous way show Thine unfailing love, O Thou, who savest those who look for refuge from their adversaries at Thy right hand."